THE 13 STEPS TO RICHES

BASED ON THE WORK BY NAPOLEON HILL IN

THINK AND GROW RICH

CREATED BY MULTI #1 INTERNATIONAL BESTSELLING AUTHOR & AWARD WINNING SPEAKER ON HABITS

ERIK "MR AWESOME" SWANSON

THE
13 STEPS TO
RICHES

Featuring
Erik Swanson & Doria Cordova

SUBCONSCIOUS
MIND VOLUME 11

HABITUDE
WARRIOR

Foreword by Dr. Anthony M. Criniti

Manufactured and printed in the United States of America and distributed globally by Beyond Publishing and Integrity Publishing International..

Hardback ISBN: 978-1-964330-23-5
Paperback ISBN: 978-1-964330-22-8

TESTIMONIALS
THE 13 STEPS TO RICHES

"What an honor to collaborate with so many personal development leaders from around the world as we Co-Author together honoring the amazing principles by Napoleon Hill in this new book series, *The 13 Steps to Riches*, by Habitude Warrior and Erik "Mr. Awesome" Swanson. Well done, "Mr. Awesome," for putting together such an amazing series. If you want to up-level your life, read every book in this series and learn to apply each of these time-tested steps and principles."

Denis Waitley ~ Author of *Psychology of Winning* & *The NEW Psychology of Winning—Top Qualities of a 21st Century Winner*

"Just as *Think and Grow Rich* reveals the 13 steps to success discovered by Napoleon Hill after interviewing the richest people around the world (and many who considered themselves failures) in the early 1900s, *The 13 Steps to Riche*s, produced by Habitude Warrior and Erik Swanson takes a modern look at those same 13 steps. It brings together many of today's personal development leaders to share their stories of how *The 13 Steps to Riches* have created and propelled their own successes. I am honored to participate and share the power of Faith in my life. If you truly want to accelerate reaching the success you deserve, read every volume of *The 13 Steps to Riches*."

Sharon Lechter ~ 5 Time N.Y. Times Bestselling Author. Author of *Think and Grow Rich for Women*, Co-Author of *Exit Rich, Rich Dad Poor Dad, Three Feet from Gold, Outwitting the Devil* and *Success and Something Greater*

"The most successful book on personal achievement ever written is now being elaborated upon by many of the world's top thought leaders. I'm honored to Co-Author this series on the amazing principles from Napoleon Hill, in *The 13 Steps to Riches*, by Habitude Warrior, Erik "Mr. Awesome" Swanson."

> *Jim Cathcart* ~ Bestselling Author of *Relationship Selling* and *The Acorn Principle*, among many others. Certified Speaking Professional (CSP) and Former President of the National Speakers Association (NSA)

"Some books are written to be read and placed on the shelf. Others are written to transform the reader, as they travel down a path of true transcendence and enlightenment. *The 13 Steps to Riches* by Habitude Warrior and Erik Swanson is the latter. Profoundly insightful, it revitalizes the techniques and strategies written by Napoleon Hill by applying a modern perspective, and a fearsome collaboration of some of the greatest minds and thought leaders from around the globe. A must-read for all of those who seek to break free of their current levels of success, and truly extract the greatness that lies within. It is an honor and a privilege to have been selected to participate, in what is destined to be the next historic chapter in the meteoric rise of many men and women around the world."

> *Glenn Lundy* ~ Husband to one, Father to 8, Automotive Industry Expert, Author of *The Morning 5*, Creator of the popular morning show "#riseandgrind," and the Founder of "Breakfast With Champions"

"How exciting to team up with the amazing Habitude Warrior community of leaders such as Erik Swanson, Sharon Lechter, John Assaraf, Denis Waitley and so many more transformational and self-help icons to bring you these timeless and proven concepts in the fields of success and wealth. *The 13 Steps to Riches* book series will help you reach your dreams and accomplish your goals faster than you have ever experienced before!"

> *Dame Marie Diamond* ~ Featured in *The Secret*, Modern-Day Spiritual Teacher, Inspirational Speaker, Feng Shui Master

"If you are looking to crystalize your mightiest dream, rekindle your passion, break through limiting beliefs and learn from those who have done exactly what you want to do - read this book! In this transformational masterpiece, *The 13 Steps to Riches*, self-development guru Erik Swanson has collected the sage wisdom and time-tested truths from subject matter experts and amalgamated it into a one-stop-shop resource library that will change your life forever!"

> *Dan Clark* ~ Speaker Hall of Fame & N.Y. Times Bestselling Author of *The Art of Significance*

"Life has always been about who you surround yourself with. I am in excellent company with this collaboration from my fellow authors and friends, paying tribute to the life-changing principles by Napoleon Hill in this amazing new book series, *The 13 Steps to Riches*, organized by Habitude Warrior's founder and my dear friend, Erik Swanson. Hill said, 'Your big opportunity may be right where you are now.' This book series is a must-read for anyone who wants to change their lives and prosper, starting now."

> *Alec Stern* ~ America's Startup Success Expert, Co-Founder of Constant Contact

"Finally a book series that encompasses the lessons the world needs to learn and apply, but in our modern day era. As I always teach my students to "Say YES, and then figure out how," I strongly urge you to do the same. Say YES to adding all of these 13 books in *The 13 Steps to Riches* book series into your success library and watch both your business as well as your personal life grow as a result."

> *Loral Langemeier* ~ 5 Time N.Y. Times Bestselling Author, Featured in *The Secret*, Author of *The Millionaire Maker* and *YES! Energy - The Equation to Do Less, Make More*

"Napoleon Hill had a tremendous impact on my consciousness when I was very young – there were very few books nor the type of trainings that we see today to lead us to success. Whenever you have the opportunity to read and harness *The 13 Steps to Riches* as they are presented in this series, be happy (and thankful) that there were many of us out there applying the principles, testing the teachings, making the mistakes, and now being offered to you in a way that they are clear, simple and concise—with samples and distinctions that will make it easier for you to design a successful life which includes adding value to others, solving world problems, and making the world work for 100% of humanity. Read on... those dreams are about to come true!"

Dame Doria Cordova ~ CEO of Money & You, Excellerated Business School, Global Business Developer, Ambassador of New Education

"Success leaves clues, and the Co-Authors in this awesome book series, *The 13 Steps to Riches*, will continue the Napoleon Hill legacy with tools, tips, and modern-day principals that greatly expand on the original masterpiece... *Think and Grow Rich*. If you are serious about living your life to the max, get this book series now!"

John Assaraf ~ Chairman & CEO NeuroGym, MrNeuroGym.com, N.Y. Times Bestselling author of *Having It All*, *Innercise*, and *The Answer*. Also featured in *The Secret*

"Over the years, I have been blessed with many rare and amazing opportunities to invest my time and energy. These opportunities require a keen eye and immediate action. This is one of those amazing opportunities for you as a reader! I highly recommend you pick up every book in this series of *The 13 Steps to Riches* by Habitude Warrior and Erik Swanson! Learn from modern-day leaders who have embraced the lessons from the great Napoleon Hill in his classic book from 1937, *Think and Grow Rich*."

Kevin Harrington ~ Original "Shark" on Shark Tank, Creator of the Infomercial, Pioneer of the 'As Seen on TV' brand, Co-Author of *Mentor to Millions*

"When you begin your journey, you will quickly learn of the importance of the first step of *The 13 Steps To Riches*. A burning desire is the start of all worthwhile achievements. Erik 'Mr. Awesome' Swanson's newest book series contains a wealth of assistance to make your journey both successful and enjoyable. Start today... because tomorrow is not guaranteed on your calendar."

Don Green ~ 45 Years of Banking, Finance & Entrepreneurship, Bestselling Author of *Everything I Know About Success I Learned From Napoleon Hill & Napoleon Hill My Mentor: Timeless Principles to Take Your Success to the Next Level & Your Millionaire Mindset*

Our minds become magnetized with the dominating thoughts we hold in our minds and these magnets attract to us the forces, the people, the circumstances of life which harmonize with the nature of our dominating thoughts.

(Napoleon Hill)

Global Speakers Mastermind & Habitude Warrior Masterminds

Join us and become a member of our tribe! Our Global Speakers Mastermind is a virtual group of amazing thinkers and leaders who meet twice a month. Sessions are designed to be 'to the point' and focused while sharing fantastic techniques to grow your mindset as well as your pocketbooks. We also include famous guest speaker spots for our private Masterclasses. We also designate certain sessions for our members to mastermind with each other & and counsel on the topics discussed in our previous Masterclasses. It's time for you to join a tribe who truly cares about **YOU** and your future and start surrounding yourself with the famous leaders and mentors of our time. It is time for you to up-level your life, businesses, and relationships.

For more information to check out our Masterminds:
Team@HabitudeWarrior.com
www.DecideToBeAwesome.com

BECOME AN INTERNATIONAL
#1 BESTSELLING AUTHOR & SPEAKER

Habitude Warrior International has been highlighting award-winning Speakers and #1 Bestselling Authors for over 25 years. They know what it takes to become #1 in your field and how to get the best exposure around the world. If you have ever considered giving yourself the GIFT of becoming a well-known Speaker and a fantastically well known #1 Best-Selling Author, then you should email their team right away to find out more information in how you can become involved. They have the best of the best when it comes to resources in achieving the bestselling status in your particular field. Start surrounding yourself with the N.Y. Times Bestsellers of our time and start seeing your dreams become reality!

For more information to become a #1 Bestselling Author
& Speaker on our Habitude Warrior Conferences
Please text the word AUTHORS to 619-304-6268
And also go to:
www.DecideToBeAwesome.com

Acknowledgement To Napoleon Hill

I would like to personally acknowledge and thank the one and only Napoleon Hill for his work, dedication, and most importantly believing in himself. His unwavering belief in himself, whether he realized this or not, had been passed down from generation to generation to millions and millions of individuals across this planet including me!

I'm sure, at first, as many of us experience throughout our lives as well, he most likely had his doubts. Think about it. Being offered to work for Andrew Carnegie for a full twenty years with zero pay and no guarantee of success had to be a daunting decision. But, I thank you for making that decision years and years ago. It paved the path for countless many who have trusted in themselves and found success in their own rights. You gave us all hope, desire, and faith to bank on the most important energy in the world—ourselves!

For this, I thank you Sir, from the bottom of my heart and the top of all of our bank accounts. Let us all follow the 13 Steps to Riches and prosper in so many areas of our lives.

~ Erik "Mr. Awesome" Swanson
13 Time #1 Bestselling Author & Student of Napoleon Hill Philosophies

Lance Cpl. Kareem M. Nikoui, 20

It is our distinct honor to dedicate each one of *The 13 Steps to Riches* book volumes to each of the 13 United States Service Members who courageously lost their lives in Kabul in August 2021. Your honor, dignity, and strength will always be cherished and remembered.

~ Habitude Warrior Team

Lance Cpl. Kareem M. Nikoui, 20, of Norco, California.

His awards and decorations include the National Defense Service Medal and the Global War on Terrorism Service Medal. Additional awards pending approval may include Purple Heart, Combat Action Ribbon, and Sea Service Deployment Ribbon. We honor you and thank you for your ultimate sacrifice!

THE 13 FEATURED CELEBRITY AUTHORS

DENIS WAITLEY ~ Author of *Psychology of Winning & The NEW Psychology of Winning—Top Qualities of a 21st Century Winner*, NASA's Performance Coach, Featured in *The Secret.* ~ www.DenisWaitley.com

SHARON LECHTER ~ 5 Time N.Y. Times Bestselling Author. Author of *Think and Grow Rich for Women*, Co-Author of *Exit Rich, Rich Dad Poor Dad, Three Feet from Gold, Outwitting the Devil* and *Success and Something Greater.* ~ www.SharonLechter.com

JIM CATHCART~ Bestselling Author of *Relationship Selling* and *The Acorn Principle*, among many others. Certified Speaking Professional (CSP) and Former President of the National Speakers Association (NSA). ~ www.Cathcart.com

MICHAEL E. GERBER ~ N.Y. Times Bestseller of the mega-bestselling theory for over two consecutive decades...*The E-Myth* Books. ~ www.MichaelEGerberCompanies.com

GLENN LUNDY ~ Husband to one, Father to 8, Automotive Industry Expert, Author of *The Morning 5*, Creator of the popular morning show "#riseandgrind," and the Founder of Breakfast With Champions. ~ www.GlennLundy.com

MARIE DIAMOND ~ Featured in *The Secret*, Modern Day Spiritual Teacher, Inspirational Speaker, Feng Shui Master.
~ www.MarieDiamond.com

DAN CLARK ~ Award Winning Speaker, Speaker Hall of Fame, N.Y. Times Bestselling Author of *The Art of Significance.*
~ www.DanClark.com

ALEC STERN ~ America's Startup Success Expert, Co-Founder of Constant Contact, Speaker, Mentor, and Investor.
~ www.AlecSpeaks.com

ERIK SWANSON ~ 13 Time #1 International Bestselling Author, Award-Winning Speaker, Featured on TEDx Talks and Amazon Prime TV. Founder & CEO of the Habitude Warrior Brand.
~ www.SpeakerErikSwanson.com

LORAL LANGEMEIER ~ 5 Time N.Y. Times Bestselling Author, Featured in *The Secret*, Author of *The Millionaire Maker* and *YES! Energy - The Equation to Do Less, Make More.*
~ www.LoralLangemeier.com

DORIA CORDOVA ~ CEO of Money & You, Excellerated Business School, Global Business Developer, Ambassador of New Education.
~ www.FridaysWithDoria.com

JOHN ASSARAF ~ Chairman & CEO NeuroGym, MrNeuroGym.com, New York Times Bestselling Author of *Having It All, Innercise,* and *The Answer.* Also featured in *The Secret.* ~ www.JohnAssaraf.com

 **KEVIN HARRINGTON** ~ Original "Shark" on the hit TV show Shark Tank, Creator of the Infomercial, Pioneer of the As Seen on TV brand, Co-Author of *Mentor to Millions.* ~ www.KevinHarrington.TV

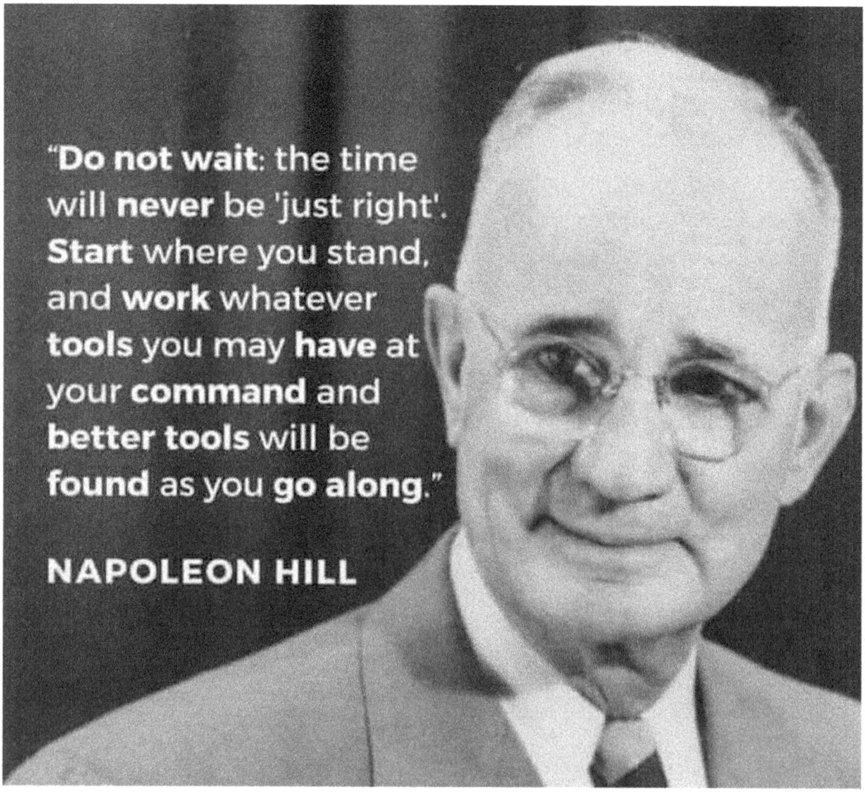

"**Do not wait**: the time will **never** be 'just right'. **Start** where you stand, and **work** whatever **tools** you may **have** at your **command** and **better tools** will be **found** as you **go along.**"

NAPOLEON HILL

THE 13 STEPS TO RICHES

CONTENTS

ERIK SWANSON & DON GREEN

Once you give yourself the gift of reading Erik Swanson's newest book series, *The 13 Steps to Riches*, you are sure to realize why he has earned his nickname, "*Mr. Awesome*." Readers usually read books for two reasons – they want to be entertained or they want to improve their knowledge in a certain subject. Mr. Awesome's new book series will help you do both.

I urge you to not only read this great book series in it's entirety, but also apply the principles held within into your our life. Use the experience Erik Swanson has gained to reach your own level of success. I highly encourage you to invest in yourself by reading self-help materials, such as *The 13 Steps to Riches*, and I truly know you will discover that it will be one of the best investments you could ever make.

Don Green
Executive Director and CEO
The Napoleon Hill Foundation

FOREWORD
BY DR. ANTHONY M. CRINITI IV

How powerful is the mind? If you are curious about the answer, please note that before you read any further, you are about to embark on a wild journey through the deepest parts of our thought machinery. I would like to introduce you to an analysis of the eleventh step to riches from *Think and Grow Rich* by Napoleon Hill. Hill holds no punches in his small chapter, discussing some of the most mysterious aspects of the subconscious mind.

The following is a sample of how deep some of Hill's conclusions reached. Hill makes the connection between the subconscious brain and Infinite Intelligence (aka "God"): "There is plenty of evidence to support the belief that the subconscious mind is the connecting link between the finite mind of man and Infinite Intelligence. It is the intermediary through which one may draw upon the forces of Infinite Intelligence at will" (Hill, 2011, p. 293). Wow! That was too powerful…you might want to read that again.

Further, Hill also explains how the connections are made from the subconscious brain and Infinite Intelligence: "The method by which you may communicate with Infinite Intelligence is very similar to that through which the vibration of sound is communicated by radio. If you understand the working principle of radio, you, of course, know that sound cannot be communicated through the ether until it has been "stepped up," or changed into a rate of vibration which the human ear cannot detect" (Hill, 2011, p. 300-301).

What role does prayer have in facilitating the communication process from our brains to the universe? Hill has an answer to that too: "Before your prayer will reach Infinite Intelligence (a statement of the author's theory only), it probably is transformed from its original thought vibration into terms of spiritual vibration. Faith is the only known agency which will give your thoughts a spiritual nature. Faith and fear make poor bedfellows. Where one is found, the other cannot exist" (Hill, 2011, p. 301).

This is one of Hill's most powerful and provocative chapters, showcasing an intensely scientific side of this amazing man. He pushes the edges on all of the conclusions in his book by elaborating on some of its most debatable topics. After reading this chapter, you might disagree with Hill and his logic, but you will certainly gain another great perspective.

This chapter covers various topics from emotions, religion, science, and the significance of thought. At the roots of the subconscious is a thought-generating machine powered by the energy in your body. Hill states: "Thoughts are truly things, for the reason that every material thing begins in the form of thought-energy" (Hill, 2011, p. 296). From these thoughts, our material world has been created and thoughts have "become things."

I encourage you to read this book, showcasing our various coauthors' perspectives of Hill's eleventh step to riches chapter. I also want to acknowledge the hard work of Erik Swanson and Jon Kovach Jr. to make this series possible. It has been a game changer for many of us coauthors to help us dig deeper and into the conclusions of such a powerful book. I also admire and appreciate Erik's foresight of connecting the featured authors in this series properly with the subjects of their expertise.

Next, I would like to acknowledge our featured celebrity author for this edition, Doria Cordova. She has been instrumental in building up one of the most successful business programs to date. Doria has been surrounded by many of the biggest names in the self-development world for decades, including various leaders in the mental sciences. I have cohosted many virtual events with Doria, and can attest that she is a wealth of knowledge. I am honored to welcome her insight on such a powerful topic.

Finally, as a coauthor of this amazing series, I encourage you to read my own personal chapter connecting the dots from the eleventh step to riches to finance and, ultimately, the problems of prosperity that humanity is facing.

In my analysis, some of the conclusions of my three books were applied to the essence of this chapter. Money, one of the major tools of finance, is after all tied to the hip of both the conscious and the subconscious mind. As stated in Principle 133 of The Most Important Lessons in Economics and Finance: "The belief in what money can do is what makes it powerful" (Criniti, 2014, p. 165). These beliefs can be found at the deepest levels of our thoughts and emotions in the abyss of our subconscious. Truly, if you want to grow rich, you must "think" first. Happy readings!

~ Dr. Anthony M. Criniti IV

References

Criniti, Anthony M., IV. 2013. *The Necessity of Finance: An Overview of the Science of Management of Wealth for an Individual, a Group, or an Organization. Philadelphia: Criniti Publishing.*

Criniti, Anthony M., IV. 2014. *The Most Important Lessons in Economics and Finance: A Comprehensive Collection of Time-Tested Principles of Wealth Management. Philadelphia: Criniti Publishing.*

Criniti, Anthony M., IV. 2016. *The Survival of the Richest: An Analysis of the Relationship between the Sciences of Biology, Economics, Finance, and Survivalism. Philadelphia: Criniti Publishing.*

Hill, Napoleon. 2011. *Think and Grow Rich. United Kingdom: Capstone Publishing Ltd.*

DR. ANTHONY M. CRINITI IV

Dr. Anthony M. Criniti IV (aka "Dr. Finance®") is the world's leading financial scientist and survivalist. A fifth-generation native of Philadelphia, Dr. Criniti is a former finance professor at several universities, a former financial planner, an active investor in diverse marketplaces, an explorer, an international keynote speaker, and has traveled around the world studying various aspects of finance. He is an Award-Winning Author of three #1 International Bestselling Finance Books: *The Necessity of Finance* (2013), *The Most Important Lessons in Economics and Finance* (2014), and *The Survival of the Richest* (2016). Dr. Criniti is also the host of the highly successful Dr. Finance® Live Podcast, as well as one of the top hosts of Clubhouse. Dr. Criniti has started a grassroots movement that is changing the way that we think about economics and finance. Learn more about Doctor Finance at *DrFinance.Info*.

www.DrFinance.info

Dame Doria Cordova

THE SUBCONSCIOUS—THE GREATEST POWER

I am so honored to be part of this publication—to have the privilege of writing about the "greatest power" for any human being, the Subconscious, and to share what I've learned in nearly five decades of personally working on myself.

Once we understand the potential benefits and drawbacks of the Subconscious and we have established firewalls and self-mastery tools to deal with it under any adverse circumstance, our level of confidence, self-trust, and self-mastery goes through the roof!

I know that I can support you in having greater success, personal power, prosperity, health, peace, and joy. I can help you to have a life where you can live in the greatest experience of them all: Sufficiency!

The Subconscious mind has been a topic of fascination and debate for centuries. It is widely known that our Subconscious thoughts and emotions play a significant role in shaping our decisions and relationships, especially in the business world—everywhere we look!

Bottom line: The Subconscious has a huge influence on our lives. Allow me to offer practical guidance on overcoming these pitfalls, fostering greater conscious awareness, and enhancing the overall quality of important decisions.

To give you a little context as to why I have "earned the right" to speak about this subject, let me share a bit about my life. Through a series of wondrous circumstances that I consciously never imagined, I became part of the team of pioneers of the entrepreneurial, experiential, transformational training industry in the late 1970s which now permeates the industry globally. This field, of course, supports people around the world to clear their Subconscious and reach the life of their dreams.

Everyone's life is affected by Generalized Principles. A Generalized Principle is always true. These are principles proven by science and physics. Whether we believe in them or not, they exist. One Generalized Principle is **gravity**; another is **leverage**; and one not so well-known but equally powerful is **precession**. Precession is the physics term for ripple effects. They are always present.

The synergy that can be created when we understand how powerfully the Subconscious affects our thoughts, behaviors, feelings, and actions, and learn to manage it, is extraordinary.

At the young age of twenty-six, through a spiritual awakening, and having attended one of the first (and most successful) human potential trainings, EST, I was blessed to learn at the time that if I couldn't have control over my circumstances (I had experienced the tremendous loss of my beloved, two miscarriages, and a dozen friends), at least I could have control of my consciousness.

I finally had a glimpse that I could have a life that could work for me with much less fear, anxiety, and stress… the possibilities were heavenly! I knew I could be financially successful. I just didn't know that I could also be personally happy and live a purpose-driven life.

Once I started putting my attention on clearing my Subconscious of negative programming, my life pivoted to what eventually led me to create the results that are evident today.

In the 1970s, there wasn't as much research as we have now. We now know that self-mastery work, exercise, breathing, healthy foods, a focus on adding value to others, being loving and kind, having integrity, and committing our lives to the betterment of humanity can bring us true happiness and joy.

As a Latina woman having accomplished the "American dream," I know that it had much to do with the values that were taught to me by my mother, auntie, grandmother, and other amazing family members that led my thinking.

And then there was the Subconscious…

I had to overcome strong beliefs, thoughts, and decisions that I had made because of my environment, as I had been literally "brainwashed" in traditional schools (as had everyone else). I had to learn Financial Literacy on my own by attending programs like the Burklyn Business School (which evolved to what I own today, the Excellerated Business School) and many programs taught by experts outside of traditional education.

I had to clear Subconscious blocks to achieve the level of success that I knew I had in me, and thank God, I realized that I actually had to raise my "deservability" level in order to allow more success, in every area of my life.

How did I do that? First, I am eternally thankful to Sondra Ray, one of the original metaphysicians who influenced many of the leaders in the industry, including myself. When I discovered that I wanted to commit myself to the betterment of humanity and attended the first Business School for Entrepreneurs of its kind that I mentioned earlier, all these negative thoughts began to literally spurt from my Subconscious. I found myself fighting beliefs that I literally didn't know I had.

She then introduced me to the "Magical Exercises" (a title that emerged after decades of personally using them, as many other leaders in our industry). I had to clear my Subconscious of the beliefs about money, business, and success that I had learned from my parents, family, school, church, books, movies, the environment—essentially, the world!

Most of humanity is programmed to believe that we live in a world of scarcity—even though the Malthusian theory of economics (the work of governments is to manage scarce resources) was proven obsolete in the early 1970s. Think about that... That was over fifty years ago! It was proven then that the world had enough resources to feed everyone, to house everyone.

The systems and tools were there to share energy sources for the world to have electricity, which is essential to eradicating poverty and hunger. We actually live in a world that has enough, yet sufficiency is one of the most fleeting experiences for so many!

If you don't believe that, your Subconscious is hard at work. And here's where the daily, moment-to-moment discipline comes into play: take three deep breaths. Feel the reaction, question what is being activated, and decide if (whatever you are feeling) is something that is worth working on so that you are the CEO of your life, and the captain of your ship. This will help you clearly and soberly make decisions that will empower you to have a successful life.

Recognize when you are in reaction. Take three deep breaths and come back to center. Do the work and find that inner family that can lead you to have more courage, more clarity, and more certainty than that which you choose, which will lead you to a better life.

I learned this very young: Just because I don't believe something, doesn't mean that it isn't true. Your beliefs will taint your reality, so that you will find the evidence necessary to make those beliefs true. You can actually see it in the division that has been created in the world today around medicine, science, and technology.

Who is running the show, you or your Subconscious? Are you aware of the beliefs that you have about the subject that you are tackling today? Do you have the correct information, facts, and what has worked in that situation? Are you willing to learn from other people's mistakes? Or are you the type that will spend the rest of your life having the same "learning experiences" (mistakes), hoping for a different outcome?

Do the *Magical Exercises* that have made a huge difference to so many who have done them. You can find them in our *www.FridaysWithDoria.com* global platform under *Resources*. Clear your Subconscious and do the daily work to create a reality that empowers you, that allows you to find the information, tools, and techniques that have worked for tens of millions to have a successful business, or organization (for-profit or non-profit).

Study those who have created extraordinary results in the area that you are interested in, or already have success in. Remember, there are **three stages of money**: **making it, keeping it, and growing it.** What stage are you in? Each stage requires for your Subconscious to have empowering beliefs every step of the way. It's the greatest power, after all.

If your Subconscious is running amok with beliefs that you have collected unchecked, you will have chaos. If you are aware of them and are CONSCIOUSLY working on them, you will have power.

"It is the Way," as they say in the *Mandalorian – Star Wars* offshoot.

Consciously increase your self-awareness. Developing a deeper understanding of your emotions, thoughts, and biases can help you recognize when they might be influencing your decision-making. Mindfulness meditation, journaling, and self-reflection exercises such as the *Magical Exercises* are effective ways to cultivate self-awareness.

I personally have practiced Transcendental Meditation (TM) for fourteen years without fail. It has been one of my greatest disciplines, and here's why.

Once you begin to have self-mastery, you will find that your intuition (gut feeling) will become more prevalent... your ability to process new information and experiences will lead you to insights that may not be immediately apparent through logical analysis. Intuition can be a valuable tool in making quick decisions or identifying potential opportunities and risks. My ability to make decisions has sped up and improved.

Your emotional intelligence will increase exponentially. You will find that certain situations that used to trigger you no longer do. Learn to manage your emotions effectively. Acknowledge and validate your emotions but avoid letting them dictate your decisions. Techniques such as emotional intelligence training, stress management, and seeking feedback from trusted mentors, colleagues, and friends can help you regulate your emotions and make more balanced decisions.

You will excel at identifying patterns and connections between seemingly unrelated pieces of information, which can lead to innovative ideas and solutions. You will have enhanced creativity. Many creative insights and ideas arise from the subconscious mind, often when we least expect them. This can lead to breakthroughs in problem-solving and the development of new products or strategies.

I recommend that you create environments that foster creativity in your business, organization, and family! Encourage brainstorming sessions, open discussions, and collaboration within your teams/family to stimulate the Subconscious mind and generate innovative ideas. Providing a safe space for experimentation and risk-taking can lead to breakthroughs in problem-solving.

Remember, the Subconscious mind wields significant influence over our business decisions and relationships. By understanding its origins and recognizing its potential benefits and drawbacks, we can develop strategies to harness its power and not only make better-informed decisions, we can also design our lives so that we actualize our most cherished heart's desires!

May the force be with you!

DAME DORIA CORDOVA

Dame Doria (DC) Cordova, PhD (Hon.) is CEO / Owner of Excellerated Business Schools® / Money & You®—the organization that brought to the world entrepreneurial, experiential, transformational training programs (now both off- and online) since 1979 with over 200,000 graduates from over eighty-five countries.

The renowned *Money & You®* program has inspired some of today's best-known business education and wealth experts, thus it has touched the lives of tens of millions globally, including through the first *Rich Dad* book, which was co-authored by her business partner of nine years, (1985 – 1994) Robert Kiyosaki.

She is a Bestselling Author. She has published the *Money & You® book series* which educates the masses with tools, techniques, and principles used by tens of millions to reach financial and personal success. In addition, she is one of the contributors to the *Think and Grow Rich for*

Women book, and the author of the comprehensive systems manual, *Money-Making Systems*.

She is a sought-after keynote speaker; and has been in countless digital events, podcasts, and films. She has been featured in many book series; and has written many forewords for books written by graduates of her programs and notable wealth, transformational leaders.

Dame Doria is a Global Business Developer for organizations that are in alignment with her purpose: *to uplift humanity's consciousness through socially responsible business.* One of her missions is to transform educational systems around the world and eradicate poverty and hunger. Another is the greening of the world. All the endeavors that she is involved in must be in alignment with those missions.

Dame Doria is a Visiting Professor at the International Micro-emission University (IMU)—the first university in the world dedicated to educating young students, professionals, entrepreneurs, and all who wish to be educated in the emerging industry of Renewables.

She is a humanitarian and philanthropist who supports numerous non-profits, foundations, and humanitarian organizations as a mentor and champion. She is now leading this work through the *Doria Cordova Foundation.*

www.MeetDoria.com

Erik Swanson

CONGRUENCY IS THE KEY FACTOR

"Act with purpose, courage, confidence, competence and intelligence until these qualities 'lock in' to your subconscious mind."
~ **Brian Tracy**

What is the real difference between the conscious mind and the subconscious mind? The conscious mind and the subconscious mind are two distinct aspects of our mental processes.

The conscious mind refers to our awareness of our thoughts, feelings, sensations, and perceptions in the present moment. It is responsible for our logical thinking, decision-making, and our ability to process information consciously. When we are consciously aware of something, we can actively focus our attention on it and direct our thoughts and actions accordingly.

On the other hand, the subconscious mind, also known as the unconscious mind, refers to the part of our mind that operates below the level of conscious awareness. It contains a vast amount of information, memories, beliefs, emotions, and instincts that influence our thoughts, feelings, and behavior. The subconscious mind is constantly active and is responsible for automatic processes such as regulating bodily functions, storing and retrieving memories, and influencing our habits and reactions.

While the conscious mind represents our immediate awareness and rational thinking, the subconscious mind plays a significant role in shaping our long-term behavior, attitudes, and beliefs. It can also influence our dreams, creative thinking, and problem-solving abilities. The subconscious mind is often associated with intuitive insights, gut feelings, and the processing of information that occurs outside of conscious awareness.

It's important to note that the relationship between the conscious and subconscious mind is complex and interconnected. Information and experiences from the subconscious mind can influence our conscious thoughts and actions, and our conscious awareness can also affect the programming and functioning of the subconscious mind.

Understanding and harnessing the power of the subconscious mind can be beneficial for personal growth, self-improvement, and overcoming certain challenges or limiting beliefs. Techniques such as hypnosis, meditation, and affirmations are often used to access and work with the subconscious mind to promote positive changes in behavior and mindset.

Benefit by Tapping into Your Subconscious Mind

Tapping into your subconscious mind can be a powerful tool for personal growth and self-improvement. I have studied this for years and years. Here are some awesome techniques that people use to access their own subconscious. Here are a few methods you can explore:

1. Meditation: Regular meditation can help you quiet your conscious mind and reach a state of relaxation where your subconscious thoughts and beliefs may become more accessible.

2. Visualization: Engaging in creative visualization exercises allows you to vividly imagine and create mental images of your goals, desires, and aspirations. This technique can help you connect with your subconscious mind and align it with your conscious intentions.

3. Affirmations: Repeating positive affirmations can help reprogram your subconscious mind by replacing negative thought patterns with empowering beliefs. Choose affirmations that resonate with you and repeat them regularly with conviction.

4. Hypnosis: Seeking the assistance of a trained hypnotherapist or using self-hypnosis techniques can help you bypass your conscious mind and access your subconscious directly. Under hypnosis, you can explore and address underlying beliefs, fears, or traumas.

5. Journaling: Writing in a journal, particularly in a free-flowing or stream-of-consciousness style, can reveal insights from your subconscious mind. By allowing your thoughts to flow onto paper without judgment or censorship, you may uncover hidden emotions, patterns, or ideas.

6. Dream Analysis: Paying attention to your dreams and keeping a dream journal can provide valuable insights into your subconscious mind. Dreams often contain symbols and metaphors that can reflect your deepest thoughts, fears, and desires.

Remember that tapping into your subconscious mind requires patience, practice, and self-reflection. It's essential to approach these techniques with an open mind and a willingness to explore your inner self. Additionally, seeking guidance from a qualified professional, such as a therapist or coach, can offer personalized support on your journey of self-discovery.

Become Congruent in Your Thoughts

Indeed, congruency is an important aspect when it comes to thoughts, beliefs, and actions. Congruency refers to the alignment or consistency between different elements within an individual's mindset and behavior. When there is congruency, there is harmony and coherence between what one thinks, says, and does.

In terms of thoughts, congruency implies that our beliefs, values, and perceptions are consistent with one another. When our thoughts are congruent, we experience a sense of integrity and clarity within our own mental framework. This internal consistency allows for a more stable and balanced perspective on life.

Furthermore, congruency extends to our actions and behaviors. It means that we align our actions with our beliefs and values. When our actions are congruent with our thoughts, we are more authentic and genuine in our interactions with others. This consistency fosters trust, as people can rely on us to act in accordance with what we profess to believe.

Congruency is also important for personal growth and self-awareness. When we identify any inconsistencies or in-congruencies within ourselves, it gives us an opportunity to reflect, reassess our beliefs, and make necessary adjustments. By striving for congruency, we can create a more coherent and integrated sense of self.

Overall, congruency in thoughts, beliefs, and actions helps us cultivate authenticity, integrity, and a stronger sense of self. It allows us to live in alignment with our values and fosters healthier relationships with others.

Tap into Your Subconscious Mind for Your Success

Tap into your subconscious mind so that you can be the director of your life. Much like a director in Hollywood movies, you, too, can direct your thoughts to be in congruency with others. This is the ultimate goal.

Allow your subconscious mind to work twenty-four hours a day, even though you are not consciously focusing on it. It's very much like a muscle. You will need to practice and train your brain to create the harmony between your conscious and subconscious minds. Once you create this harmony, success starts to flow in every area of your life. It's your time to take control.

ERIK SWANSON

As an Award-Winning International Keynote Speaker and 13 Time #1 Bestselling Author, Erik "Mr. Awesome" Swanson is in great demand around the world! He speaks to an average of more than one million people per year. He can be seen on Amazon Prime TV in the very popular show *SpeakUP TV*. Mr. Swanson has the honor to have been invited to speak to many universities, such as the University of California (UCSD), Cal State University, University of Southern California (USC), Grand Canyon University (GCU), and the Business and Entrepreneurial School of Harvard University.

He is also a Faculty Member of CEO Space International and is a recurring keynoter at Vistage Executive Coaching. Erik also joins the Ted Talk Family with his latest TEDx speech called "A Dose of Awesome."

Erik got his start in the self-development world by mentoring directly under the infamous Brian Tracy. Quickly climbing to become the top trainer around the world from a group of over 250 hand-picked trainers, Erik started to surround himself with the best of the best and soon started to be invited to speak on stages alongside such greats as Jim Rohn, Bob Proctor, Les Brown, Sharon Lechter, Jack Canfield, and Joe Dispenza... just to name a few.

Erik has created and developed the super-popular Habitude Warrior Conference, which has a two-year waiting list and includes 33 top-named speakers from around the world. It is a 'Ted Talk' style event that has quickly climbed to one of the top 10 events not to miss in the United States! He is the creator, founder, and CEO of the Habitude Warrior Mastermind and Global Speakers Mastermind. His motto is clear... "NDSO!": No Drama – Serve Others!

www.SpeakerErikSwanson.com

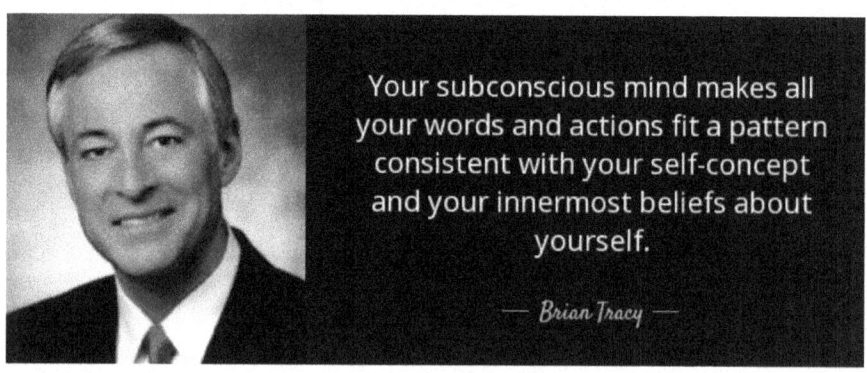

Your subconscious mind makes all your words and actions fit a pattern consistent with your self-concept and your innermost beliefs about yourself.

— Brian Tracy —

Jon Kovach Jr.

UNLEASHING WITHIN: NURTURING AN ABUNDANT SUBCONSCIOUS MIND

We live in a realm of boundless possibilities, where the subconscious mind holds the key to achieving riches beyond measure. In this chapter, inspired by Napoleon Hill's eleventh step to riches found in *Think and Grow Rich*, we venture on a journey to explore the profound influence of the subconscious mind on our path to success. Tap into the subconscious and harness its formidable power.

The Mighty Subconscious Mind

Within the intricate tapestry of human history lies the ever-awakened and relentless timekeeper—the subconscious mind. As we delve into the teachings of the *13 Steps to Riches* series, we encounter the concept of autosuggestion, which instills success-driven habits, setting us on the path to effortless achievement.

The subconscious mind serves as the conductor of this energy, meticulously recording, observing, and assimilating information. Equaling, if not surpassing, the power of the conscious mind, the subconscious acts as the linchpin completing the chapters of prosperity. Imagine journeying through life without socks in your heavy boots—it would be filled with discomfort and challenges.

Transition to Positivity, Success, & Wealth

Embarking on the transition to a world of positivity, success, and wealth is a noble pursuit. Still, it may encounter friction if the foundation resembles a tattered or mismatched sock. While transformation can occasionally happen overnight for a fortunate few, such instances are exceptions. To attain riches beyond measure, one must train the subconscious mind—the natural man—to embrace the reality of desired achievements, effectively invoking the law of attraction, or as I prefer to call it, the law of magnetism. Like attracts like, and by building a foundation of positive magnets, we create a harmonious environment to attract the outcomes we seek.

In my last chapter on Transmutation, I talked about the power of recharging. Some of the messages shared in that chapter include powerful white noise and success frequencies that, while in the background, trick the subconscious mind into believing it's being healed and restored. I'm not saying we must be tricky and sinister in developing solid access to our subconscious minds, but that there are techniques for developing a positive, powerful, and prosperous mind on autopilot.

Fueling the Subconscious Mind

It's vital to the achievement of your goals, loves, and desires that you fuel your mind, body, soul, intellect, and spirit with only the nutrients and vitamins that can scope it into your desires. Any material that is a process or fabrication of the actual nutrients will delay and even stunt the progress of success.

It's funny that a jockey and racehorse owner will feed their champion racehorse with only the most excellent nutrients and food, fueling the thoroughbred with the proper proteins that lead to winning the races. Meanwhile, the jockey and owner are so focused on giving those good ingredients to their horse that they leave the stables and head to the steakhouse, where they suck back a pint of alcohol, fatty foods, and sugars that aren't good for their own bodies.

This is a bit hypocritical if you ask me. Shouldn't we follow suit? Why do we expect greatness from others but are lenient on our own disciplines? One of the best ways to improve, enhance, and strengthen your subconscious mind is to stop worrying about others and take an inventory and hyper-focused evaluation of yourself.

Fueling the subconscious mind with positivity and prosperity is crucial for achieving desired outcomes. Just as athletes feed their bodies with the finest nutrients for peak performance, we must nourish our minds, souls, intellect, and spirits with the correct information and beliefs to manifest our desires. Any counterfeit or processed information only delays or hinders progress toward success. Maintaining consistency in providing our subconscious with the nutrients it craves is essential, aligning our actions with our aspirations.

Patience & Persistence

In the world of public relations, there is a process to identify any organization's potential reach and growth by objectively looking at its goals, mission, and objectives and then detailing the strategies and tactics to achieve the desired results. Although you cannot predict the future and human behavior, when one person sees the desired outcome and refers engineers, tactics, strategies, and processes that go into making those results, anyone can unveil the skeleton that holds the livelihood of their desires. The subconscious mind is one of the significant steps to riches because it is the underdog in any story. It is the Cinderella to your goals and dreams. If you sleep on the underdog, he can get you in the long run.

Another critical ingredient to fueling your subconscious is your belief system. Although fear can be a motivator, it's crucial to exercise the muscle of faith, so that there is no reason to alter the path. I've seen so many of my colleagues and peers pivot their lives and careers because they didn't reach the goal they set for themselves in a given timeline (usually too short of a timeline). I believe it's not because they failed on their path to success, which is why they pivoted, but that they shifted because they weren't clear on their direction. If they left the door open for a possible pivot and alteration, they left it open for the subconscious mind to accumulate a lifetime of believing that there might be Plan B's and C's and D's.

If you could trick the subconscious mind into training you to do things that don't achieve your goals, would you be able to swing the pendulum and do the exact opposite to attract the subconscious mind into achieving what you want to achieve? It seems so simple to me.

Success is a simple yet demanding process that requires consistent effort and discipline. Patience is a virtue that many undervalue, often seeking quick fixes or pivoting prematurely in their journey—Napoleon Hill's analogy of stopping three feet from gold rings true in this context. Impatience can derail progress, hindering the accumulation of positive habits in the subconscious mind. Learning from past mistakes, I recognized the importance of patience during my athletic journey and how impatience could lead to missed opportunities.

One of the saddest days of my life was when my impatience got the best of me, and my subconscious accumulation of impatient habits led to me losing the state championship in the 800-meter dash in 2008. I admit that my lack of discipline, short-cutting stretches, strengthening and conditioning, and nutritional habits led to me physically peaking too early in the season so as not to reach that state of winning at the end of my season.

I remember competing in the regional championships as one of Colorado's top-ranked 800m runners, ready to get my free ticket to State. My impatience led to me thinking that if I didn't do something drastic, I wouldn't win. I acted out of character and sprinted to the finish line too early, and my body hit a proverbial wall. It had been waiting to hit because the fuel I gave it was inadequate for the level of performance I was seeking to accomplish. Like putting diesel in a non-diesel engine, my body collapsed, and as I struggled to cross the finish line; I saw my competitors and teammates even pass me before I stumbled across the finish line.

I lost my invitation to the state championships and ultimately didn't get a shot at winning the gold medal. I had said to myself years prior,

"Although devastating, this reality has given me a lot of insight into the proper habits and the patience that goes into fueling the subconscious mind."

Every Drop Counts

After my significant loss and while taking a sabbatical from my athletics, I dedicated two years to serve an ecclesiastical Christian mission in the Philippines for my church. While filling up my mission vehicle with gas at a Chevron in the middle of the Philippine province of Cavite, I saw a billboard advertisement sign that showed a picture of the gasoline pump dripping a couple of gasoline droplets. The advertisement said, "Every drop counts." I remember these words in the ad profoundly influencing my transition and belief system.

Every drop counts, which means my lackadaisical approach to abundance can be as bad as overdosing on poison. The awakened mind is so sharp and so intelligent. But the wandering human living life, guided by the reins that pull them, will ultimately never feel the alert satisfaction of achievement that our brains and subconscious mind have the power to give. I recently talked about Transmutation as one of nature's most extraordinary powers. Still, the only physical and tangible force that can harness those powers is the belief in the mind that turning decisions into action creates autosuggestion and success on autopilot.

Similar to the significance of every drop of fuel in a race car, every ounce of belief and positive reinforcement counts in shaping the subconscious mind. Our subconscious keeps an unwavering score, tallying each drop contributing to our success. Just as we wouldn't pour diesel into a non-diesel engine or feed unhealthy substances to a racing horse champion, we should prioritize providing our subconscious with the correct fuel—positive beliefs, nourishing thoughts, and unwavering faith.

I don't just learn from my mistakes. Here's a positive example of a triumphant performance: On the 100th episode of the Circle of Knowledge podcast, my self-made podcast show, which I have hosted since 2016, I interviewed one of my all-time heroes and admired legends.

Joining me on the show was the greatest Canadian pole vaulter of all time (G.C.P.V.O.A.T.), Alysha Newman. I've had many interviews with successful champions, Olympic athletes, and Hall of Famers. Still, this one, in particular, was a great deal to me because after 600-plus hours of interviews with successful people, talking and inquiring about the habits and success tips of champions, it occurred to me, mid-interview with one of my heroes, that this is one of the best interviews I have ever performed. It was so natural; it felt like I was hosting the Tonight Show with Jimmy Fallon, and the transition was so smooth.

I built a connection and a friendship with this elite athlete, for whom I have so much admiration and respect. As we talked about the power of mindset, Alysha stressed the importance of putting what the body needs in your body for success. Go to any bodybuilder, elite athlete, or champion, and ask them if their diet and nutrition are equal to the importance of the information and quality of intellect with which they surround themselves.

Alysha spoke of her own life of insecurities and doubts and inner demons that got in her way from many championships and competitions. By eliminating those distractions from her life, focusing on every ounce and drop of fuel, she became the world's greatest pole vaulter. She has achieved things that no other pole vaulter has accomplished before. I remember sitting in the interview thinking to myself, "Wow, this is one of my best interviews." It was.

I walked away from the interview with a lifelong friend, tremendous respect and connection for one of the most outstanding athletes in the world, and a better understanding of what it takes to be a champion. Every drop counts, which means every ounce of nutrition, positivity, and belief accumulates to success. The subconscious mind keeps score, constantly listening to these drops. You would not put diesel in a non-diesel tank. You would not feed the wrong foods to a thoroughbred racing horse champion. Why would you do it to yourself?

Take the initiative, be disciplined, and if you can do something for a minute, you can do something for another minute. If you can do something for an hour, you can do it for another hour. If you can do something for a day, you can do it another day. And that continues to snowball into a lifetime and even seasons of more incredible achievement and success. I am in a current state of recharge, and I am grateful for the reminders of success and how the anatomy of a champion is built on every ounce and every drop that counts.

The Power of Better Choices

It's funny that one of my favorite personal development books is a nutrition book. Although I'm not a health geek and an elite athlete anymore, nor do I follow the book's teachings to a T, it has had a profound message that gives me better food for thought and my subconscious mind. The book is called *How Not to Die* by Dr. Michael Greger. The renowned doctor has discovered, through research, an extensive study that increased consumption of vegetables can decrease symptoms of many diseases and eliminate them. From diabetes to Alzheimer's, there is a cure through repetitive consumption of the proper nutrition, and most doctors are sleeping on the idea that this is possible because they were raised in a society where drugs and medication can be the quick fixes to the ailments most humans desire.

Dr. Gregor encourages us all to live a life of increased consumption of vegetables, even when we do not rely on various substances, such as meats, dairy products, and sugar. Those three things seem to be the leading cause of many diseases.

However, what is so profound is that Dr. Gregor teaches us the principles of good, better, and best choices. For a palpable example, a good choice would be to have a salad on the side of your plate of lasagna. The better option would be to limit the carbs and meat on that lasagna and have a more fantastic salad. You are still enjoying the lasagna, just increasing the consumption of vegetables.

However, the best choice would be to have a plant-based lasagna recipe, no meat, no processed foods, sitting on a large bed of dark greens and vibrating carotene and vegetables. If you can make better decisions, you're already decreasing the odds of disease. And by making the best choices, you accelerate the results of magnified nutrition and improve your odds of eliminating diseases.

It's essential to apply these principles not just to your plate at dinner and breakfast but to choose good versus better versus best choices with everything you do towards success and riches. Just by writing this chapter, I already believe in your success. I am excited to see the results as I believe there are other people out there, not as far along as you and I, waiting for us to reach the finish line so that we can turn around and cheer them on through their race journey.

It's not about achieving personal success. It's more important to achieve personal success so that we can help others achieve their own success so that they can, in turn, help others. You have the tools and the resources. The train is already in motion. Your subconscious mind has what it needs. Continue from this point forward to fuel it with every ounce drop of pure nutrition towards success. If you can do it for a day, you can do it for a week. If you can do it for a week, you can do it for a month. And if you can do it for a month, you're unstoppable.

By embracing the "good, better, best" principle, we can make conscious decisions toward success in every aspect of life. Like opting for a healthier meal choice, we should consistently choose the best options for our subconscious mind. The subconscious thrives on these elevated choices, propelling us toward our desired outcomes. When we embrace the power of our subconscious, we achieve personal success and inspire and uplift others on their journeys.

Remember that your subconscious mind holds the key to unlimited potential. By nurturing it with positive beliefs, persistent efforts, and unwavering patience, you create a fertile ground for prosperity and abundance. Fuel every ounce and drop of your being with the nutrients of success, and watch as your subconscious mind guides you toward achieving your dreams. Embrace the power within, and, in doing so, become a beacon of inspiration for others, igniting a ripple effect of achievement and triumph across the world.

JON KOVACH JR

About Jon Kovach Jr.: Jon is an award-winning international motivational speaker and global mastermind leader. Jon has helped multi-billion-dollar corporations, including Coldwell Banker Commercial, Outdoor Retailer Cotopaxi, and the Public Relations Student Society of America, exceed their annual sales goals. In addition, in his work as an accountability coach and mastermind facilitator, Jon has helped thousands of professionals overcome their challenges and achieve their goals by implementing his accountability strategies and Irrefutable Laws of High Performance. Jon is the Founder and Chairman of Champion Circle, a networking association that combines high-performance-based networking activities and recreational fun to create connection capital and increase prosperity for professionals. Jon is the Mastermind Facilitator and Team Lead of the Habitude Warrior Mastermind and the Global Speakers Mastermind & Masterclass founded by Speaker Erik "Mr. Awesome" Swanson.

Jon speaks on topics including accountability, The Irrefutable Laws of High Performance, and The Power of Mastermind Methodologies. He is a #1 Bestselling Author and a featured keynote on *SpeakUp TV*, an Amazon Prime TV series, with his keynote speech titled, Getting Unstuck. In addition, he stars in over 100 speaking stages, podcasts, and live international summits each year. Jon's motivational messages have been viewed by over 500,000 people online. His positive messages have trended and been used by global brands on TikTok and Instagram, such as: Red Bull, Michael Bublé, NHL, Powell Books, GoDaddy Studio, Canada's Wonderland Amusement Park, and the LSU Cheer Team.

Author's Website: *www.JonKovachJr.com*

Book Series Website: *www.The13StepsToRiches.com*

Amado Hernandez

NETWORK OF CHAMPIONS NOW & ITS CAST

"Do not conform to the pattern of this world but be transformed by the renewing of your mind."
~ **Romans 12:2**

"I WILL CHANGE THE WORLD AND CREATE HUGE WEALTH" popped up on my Facebook feed under the name of one of my "friends." In the background was a photo of a bright orange exotic car. I have never had a bright orange exotic car and am not sure what make and model it was. And, since the photo was watermarked with "gettyimages©," my Facebook friend may have not known the make and model of the bright orange exotic car, either.

"I will change the world and create huge wealth" is an amazing proclamation. It sounds like a modern-day answer to a beauty pageant question, "What makes you different from other contestants?" Changing the world and creating huge wealth is an accomplishment that most of us would love to achieve during our lifetimes. I can't think of a better nine-word affirmation.

The challenge for my Facebook friend, and for most of us, is how to transform dreams into reality. Anyone can post their dreams, aspirations, and affirmations on Facebook along with real or imagined confirmations of their power, wealth, and success. But it takes more to make wishes, hopes, and dreams come true.

There was a time in America, before the pandemic—maybe even long before the pandemic—that most of us believed in "The American Dream." For some, "The American Dream" meant working at a factory or store or maybe even owning a business until, someday, they could buy the house of their dreams. They pictured their dream home with its white picket fence, well-groomed lawn, and bright blooming flowers.

But more than that, they pictured themselves and their families inside their homes. They thought about how they would *feel* being safe and happy and comfortable. They dreamed of birthday parties, Thanksgiving dinners, and Christmas trees with gifts being opened by happy kids and grandkids and maybe even great grandkids. All those visions of sugarplums, even tamales, filling their subconscious minds.

And that, in the final analysis, is the power of the subconscious mind. There is more to *Think and Grow Rich* than just "thinking" and that's why Napoleon Hill included "Chapter 12: The Subconscious Mind" in *Think and Grow Rich.* A lot has changed in America since Napoleon Hill published his book in 1937 but the power of the subconscious mind holds tried and true.

There are two different—but not necessarily distinct—elements of "The American Dream." Correlated to *home ownership* is *business ownership.* The challenges of the pandemic with its lingering damage to our global economy have created an environment of *fading dreams and rising fears.* For many, "The American Dream"—in pre- or post-pandemic life—has become as elusive as grabbing the brass ring in the nose of a carousel horse as it keeps passing by on a Merry-Go-Round somewhere in Fantasyland.

My challenge as an entrepreneur and real estate professional is to educate, empower, and inspire others to continue reaching for those brass rings of *home ownership* and *business ownership.* The reason I have done that for many decades is that I continue to believe in God, America, and "The American Dream." And that brings us right to *the subconscious mind.*

I just told you *why* I do what I do: because I believe in "The American Dream" and believe that God gifted me the vision, skills, and passion to help others achieve *their own* American Dream—whatever that may mean to them.

If *thinking* is not enough to help us grab those brass rings, what is? Without getting into topics like Quantum Physics and Epigenetics, I am going to explain exactly what we need to do and how to do it. Our minds are the most powerful computers in the world. Our subconscious mind is like the hard drive in a computer. It has been programmed since the moment we were conceived. It is continually programmed and reprogrammed 24/7 each and every day of our lives from womb to tomb.

Unfortunately, and often tragically, most of our programming can be negative, toxic, limiting, paralyzing, and self-sabotaging. Society inputs most of our programs—from media and social media; from friends and family; from business associates and competitors. It all comes into our subconscious minds *raw, unplugged, and unfiltered.* Virtually all the programming is designed around using fear to manipulate and control us.

Ninety percent of our lives is influenced—and may be controlled—by outside programming. Most of us allow our subconscious mind to be programmed, reprogrammed, and even updated by others. We must *take control* of our conscious and subconscious minds to break free and live the lives that we want to live.

Traditionally, we have been programmed to *work hard,* believing that someday, usually at age sixty five, we can retire with no mortgage, a pension, Social Security Income, and a retirement plan. At age sixty five, we can stop working and start enjoying our lives. Ten thousand Americans are turning age sixty five each day and many can't afford to stop working. If they didn't lose their jobs, businesses, or homes during the pandemic, they are living week-to-week or maybe even day-to-day.

We are in turbulent times when people are worried about where they are going to get money or healthcare or maybe when, how, and where they can even live. They have allowed the government, media, and society to manipulate them into a box where they are trapped, afraid, confused, overwhelmed, and defeated.

By reprogramming our subconscious minds, and continually upgrading our mental software and firmware, we can instantly and dramatically change our lives. In a more general sense, we need to delete toxic people, time wasters, limiting beliefs, and negative feelings and emotions from our minds. How do we do that? That's the operative question.

Until we take control of our own minds, we will continue to be manipulated and exploited by others. We will continue to be overwhelmed and afraid. If we don't control ourselves, we will always be controlled by others. Here are the three steps you can do NOW to reprogram your mind, break free, and live the life you deserve to live.

First, invest a few hours in yourself to decide how you are going to jump out of the conga line and dance your own dance. Forget about competing with everyone's Facebook selfies and "likes" and start loving yourself and begin caring for yourself. Programming begins with loving yourself and realizing that you are enough and deleting self-limiting beliefs and corrupted files from your subconscious mind—your mind is your hard drive.

These turbulent times are temporary—just like everything else we have gone through. It's important to recognize and keep in mind that the battle is not with inflation, interest rates, gas prices, or even with our business competitors. Our battles are internal—they are fought deep within our own hearts, minds, and souls. The forces of evil, weapons of mass destruction, monsters of our pain, fears, and failures lurk deep within us.

What do you do when you get a new smartphone or computer? And what do you do when your devices stop working because they have been hacked or the files have been corrupted? You start erasing files, cleaning your hard drive, and maybe even resetting the device to factory settings. Think about that—reset your mind to the "factory settings" you had when you were born. Remember when you were a kid? The sun was hot, but not too hot? Rain was wet, but not too wet? Balloons and kites and toys were fun.

Second, make a one-page plan for programming, reprogramming, and upgrading your mind every day.

Third, and finally, TAKE ACTION. All the plans, vision boards, affirmations, motivational videos, and success books—and even the mental programming—in the world will do nothing unless you take immediate, massive, and consistent action. Without action, a definite chief aim, a simple plan, and constantly positively programming your mind, you'll continue to underperform or even fail.

Remember that every thought you have, every move you make, and every word you speak automatically updates your mental hard drive. Remain conscious of that. Know *why* you are doing what you're doing, *why* you're saying what you're saying, and diligently guard the quality, intent, and integrity of every thought.

I know why, how, and when to program and upgrade my subconscious mind. Do you? Emerge yourself in knowledge and surround yourself with inspiring minds. That's how to change your life and the lives of others—and maybe even "change the world and create huge wealth." Let me know which make and model of a bright orange exotic car you choose!

AMADO HERNANDEZ

About Amado Hernandez: Amado was born in Mexico of humble beginnings and raised in Los Angeles, California. As an avid reader, Amado always focused on self-development. He coaches sales professionals to make six and seven figures in real estate.

Amado believes in a progressive culture, a people-centric culture where clients' dreams come true and salespeople thrive; at the end of the day, we all want to be respected and pursue our happiness. My goal is to leave a legacy-making a difference in people's lives.

With thirty-three years of Real Estate experience, Mr. ABC Amado Hernandez successfully operates and grows his Excellence Empire Real Estate Moreno Valley office. Broker/Owner Amado first opened his doors in 1995, and Excellence currently has over sixty offices in Southern California, Las Vegas, Merida Yucatan, Mexico, and over 1,000 Agents.

He is also part owner of a highly successful Mortgage company, Excellence Mortgage, and owner of Empire Escrow Services. Mr. Amado is also involved with his community and currently serves as Director at Inland Valley Association of Realtors and will be the President-Elect for 2023. Amado serves as a Director of CAR (California Association of Realtors).

Author's Website: *www.ExcellenceEmpireRE.com*

Book Series Website: *www.The13StepsToRiches.com*

Angelika Ullsperger

REDIRECTING THOUGHTS & EMOTIONS

How can we use transmutation to achieve a higher level of success? Well, first, we must understand what transmutation is and how it works before we can look at it in action. Napoleon Hill defines transmutation as the process of converting negative thoughts and emotions into positive ones and notes that this process is an important key to success.

The first step in the process of transmutation, according to Hill, is to acknowledge negative thoughts and emotions. He advises against denying or suppressing them, as this can lead to them becoming stronger and more pervasive. Instead, he suggests that individuals should confront their negative thoughts and emotions head-on, examine their origins, and try to understand why they are experiencing them.

The second step in the process of transmutation is to replace negative thoughts and emotions with positive ones. Hill suggests using affirmations, visualization, and positive self-talk to achieve this.

Affirmations are statements that individuals repeat to themselves to reinforce positive beliefs and behaviors. Visualization involves mentally imagining oneself achieving their goals and experiencing positive emotions. Positive self-talk is the practice of consciously directing one's thoughts in a positive direction.

Hill emphasizes that the process of transmutation requires persistence and repetition. It takes time and effort to change ingrained patterns of negative thinking and behavior. However, he also notes that the rewards of transmutation are significant. By converting negative thoughts and emotions into positive ones, individuals can harness their energy and creativity, leading to greater success in all areas of their lives. Hill cites many examples of individuals who have successfully used the process of transmutation to achieve success. For example, Andrew Carnegie rose from humble beginnings to become one of the wealthiest individuals in the world. Carnegie attributed his success to his ability to transmute negative thoughts and emotions into positive ones, which allowed him to focus on his goals and achieve them.

The concept of transmutation is a powerful tool for achieving success.

By acknowledging and confronting negative thoughts and emotions and replacing them with positive ones, individuals can harness their energy and creativity to achieve their goals. While the process of transmutation requires persistence and effort, the rewards are significant, as evidenced by the many successful individuals who have used this technique to achieve their dreams.

So, let's explore this idea by taking a look at the story of my friend, Sarah.

Sarah had a dream of starting her own business. She had a life-long passion for baking, and she yearned to open a bakery that offered unique and delicious treats. Opening this bakery had been her dream since childhood.

However, for as long as she could remember, she worked jobs she hated just to get by. Sarah was plagued by many negative thoughts and emotions that held her back. She was afraid that her business would fail, and she worried that she wasn't skilled enough to make her dream a reality. All of these thoughts weighed on her, making it difficult for her to take action and move forward with her plans.

One day, Sarah came across *Think and Grow Rich* and the concept of transmutation. The idea of converting negative thoughts and emotions into positive ones intrigued her, and she decided to give it a try.

At first, it was hard for Sarah to confront her negative thoughts and emotions. She found herself feeling overwhelmed by her fears and doubts. Oftentimes, she wanted to give up. However, as she persisted in her efforts, she began to notice a change.

Instead of feeling paralyzed by her negative thoughts, Sarah began to feel more energized and motivated. She started to see her fears and doubts as challenges that she could overcome, rather than obstacles that would hold her back.

Sarah also began using affirmations, visualization, and positive self-talk to reinforce her positive beliefs and behaviors. She repeated to herself that she was capable of starting a successful bakery, and she visualized herself running a thriving business. She also directed her thoughts in a positive direction, focusing on the steps she needed to take to make her dream a reality.

Over time, Sarah's efforts paid off. She was able to secure funding for her business, and she opened her bakery to much success. Her unique and delicious treats quickly gained a following, and she found herself busy with orders and customers.

Looking back, Sarah realized that the process of transmutation had been essential to her success. By confronting and converting her negative thoughts and emotions into positive ones, she was able to overcome her fears and doubts and make her dream a reality.

From that point on, Sarah continued to use the process of transmutation to overcome any challenges that came her way. She became a successful business owner, and her bakery became a beloved part of the community. Her story serves as a reminder that with persistence and effort, anyone can achieve their dreams by harnessing the power of transmutation.

Brain plasticity refers to the brain's ability to change and adapt in response to experiences, learning, and behavior. This concept is based on the idea that the brain is not fixed or unchangeable, but rather malleable and capable of forming new neural connections throughout one's lifetime.

So, what concepts are behind the magic of transmutation? One of the key aspects is neuroplasticity. Neuroplasticity is the brain's ability to change its physical structure in response to new experiences, learning, and behavior. Neuroplasticity allows the brain to form new connections between neurons and to strengthen existing connections, enabling us to learn new skills, change our behavior, and adapt to new situations.

The concept of transmutation is, in part, based on the principles of neuroplasticity. By consciously redirecting our thoughts and emotions towards positive ones, we can create new neural pathways that reinforce positive beliefs and behaviors.

For example, when we practice affirmations or positive self-talk, we are actively stimulating the prefrontal cortex, the part of the brain responsible for executive functioning, decision-making, and emotional regulation. The repetition of positive statements creates new neural connections in the prefrontal cortex, strengthening our ability to regulate our emotions and make positive decisions.

Similarly, visualization is a powerful tool for harnessing the brain's plasticity. When we visualize ourselves achieving a desired outcome, we activate the same neural networks that would be activated if we were actually performing the action. This helps to reinforce the neural connections associated with the behavior we want to develop, making it easier for us to perform the action in real life.

Finally, the process of transmutation is also based on the principle of cognitive reappraisal, which involves reinterpreting a situation or emotion in a positive way. This technique is based on the idea that the brain's emotional response to a situation is influenced by the way we interpret it. By consciously reframing negative situations in a positive light, we can change the way our brain responds to them, reducing feelings of stress and anxiety.

In summary, the concept of transmutation works because it is based on the principles of brain plasticity and neuroplasticity. By consciously redirecting our thoughts and emotions towards positive ones, we can create new neural pathways that reinforce positive beliefs and behaviors. This helps us to regulate our emotions, make positive decisions, and achieve our goals, ultimately leading to greater success and happiness.

ANGELIKA ULLSPERGER

About Angelika Ullsperger: Angelika is a serial entrepreneur from Baltimore, Maryland. She is a fashion designer, model, artist, photographer, and musician. Angelika has extensive and well-rounded professional experience, having worked as a business owner, carpenter, chef, graphic designer, manager, event planner, sales and product specialist, marketer, and coach. Angelika is now a #1 Bestselling Author in the historic book series, *The 13 Steps to Riches*. She is a life-long learner with a sincere and genuine interest in all things of the world with a major interest in the formal subject of abnormal psychology, neuroscience, and quantum physics.

Angelika prides herself as someone who has saved lives as a friend, first responder, EMT, and knowledgeable suicide prevention advocate. With a vast knowledge and experience in multiple professions, Angelika is also a proud honorable member of Phi Theta Kappa, The APA, the AAAS, and an FBLA (Future Business Leaders Association) Business Competition Finalist. She is Certified in basic coding and blockchain technology. Amongst the careers and vast experience, Angelika is an adventurer and avid dog lover.

Her ultimate goals and dreams are to make a lasting positive impact in people's lives through her wealth of knowledge and skillsets.

Author's Website: *www.Angelika.world*

Book Series Website: *www.The13StepsToRiches.com*

Dr. Anthony M. Criniti IV

THINKING OUTSIDE THE BOX

Think and Grow Rich by Napoleon Hill is one of the best classic books to teach someone about how to become a financial success (as well as a success in other areas of life). Within the book's pages, you will find his thirteen steps to riches; each one has its own separate chapter and analysis. The subject of our book is to interpret his eleventh step to riches: The Subconscious Mind. Let's review some of the major highlights of this chapter.

This short chapter covers a variety of subjects ranging from the subconscious mind to emotions, and even religion. First, let's start with Hill's view of what the subconscious mind is. He says: "The subconscious mind consists of a field of consciousness, in which every impulse of thought that reaches the objective mind through any of the five senses, is classified and recorded, and from which thoughts may be recalled or withdrawn as letters may be taken from a filing cabinet" (Hill, 2011, p. 292).

With this viewpoint, it is not hard to make the leap to visualize human beings as an advanced robot with no off switch; our brains are similar to a motherboard and storage unit of a computer. Hill views our subconscious as something that is always on and constantly absorbing data from all around us. When we think of our memory, we often think of remembering images and sounds. However, we can also remember the smells, tastes, and feelings of certain moments too. Our ability to remember this detailed level of stimuli demonstrates how powerful our brains really are.

Hill views the subconscious as so powerful that it might be the link that connects to a superior being(s). If you wanted to speak with God (or its equivalent—Hill labels it "Infinite Intelligence"), then this is the part of the brain that calls God (basically through what we say is "prayer"). Hill elaborates: "There is plenty of evidence to support the belief that the subconscious mind is the connecting link between the finite mind of man and Infinite Intelligence. It is the intermediary through which one may draw upon the forces of Infinite Intelligence at will" (Hill, 2011, p. 293).

Hill then expands on how speaking to the universe is similar to the way sounds are communicated by radio: "The method by which you may communicate with Infinite Intelligence is very similar to that through which the vibration of sound is communicated by radio. If you understand the working principle of radio, you of course, know that sound cannot be communicated through the ether until it has been "stepped up," or changed into a rate of vibration which the human ear cannot detect" (Hill, 2011, p. 300-301).

If the subconscious is so powerful that it is able to record and process all that we do as well as possibly communicate with "Infinite Intelligence," then it is certainly something that we would want to protect. After all, as Hill states: "For the present, it is sufficient if you remember that you are living *daily*, in the midst of all manner of thought impulses which are reaching your subconscious mind, without your knowledge" (Hill, 2011, p. 294). Master marketers know the power of the subconscious very well. They create advertisements and marketing campaigns targeting that part of the brain by giving people subtle messages to buy their products and services.

Therefore, it becomes our scared duty to build up a strong defense system to allow only what we choose to enter our minds, particularly those thoughts that will have a positive effect on our being.

Do thoughts become things? According to Hill: "Everything which man creates, begins in the form of a thought impulse. Man can create nothing which he does not first conceive in thought" (Hill, 2011, p. 295). I concur with this point that Hill has stressed in various forms throughout this book. In my own field, I have revolutionized the way that finance and economics is viewed starting from a single thought: searching for the definition of finance. This led to my quest to define economics, which led to my desire to define science. As stated in my first book *The Necessity of Finance*: "…science is a persistent search for a truly better way to perform an action or understand a condition, process, or thing" (Criniti, 2013, p. 3-4). With this definition, I was able to build more thoughts that would eventually turn into things.

The following is a rough sketch of how thoughts became things for *The Necessity of Finance*. First, the thought of properly arguing that finance is a separate science was materialized after deep thought of how to connect the definitions of both science and finance together. Second, these thoughts built the foundation to the physical book that was published, which became a #1 international bestseller sold all over the world. Finally, these chains of thoughts led to an army of ideas that opened a road to incredible discoveries found in my second and third books. Thoughts truly become things.

Hill also added an important discussion on emotions to this chapter. As the subconscious records our feelings as well, it is worth exploring the various types of emotions and their impact on our minds. Hill categorized emotions into seven major positive and negative forms. One of his key conclusions was: "Remember, in this connection, that you are studying a book that is intended to help you develop a "money consciousness" by *filling your mind with positive emotions*. One does not become money conscious by filling one's mind with negative emotions… *Positive and negative emotions cannot occupy the mind at the same time*. One or the other must dominate" (Hill, 2011, p. 298).

Hill's conclusions are very important for personal growth. It is also important to add to this discussion the collective emotion that is felt by society at any given moment, particularly due to economic conditions. Ironically, at the timing of this writing, we are in a period that I have called The Great Pandemic Depression since early 2020 when the pandemic began. Similar to the Great Depression that was the backdrop to the timeframe when Hill wrote *Think and Grow Rich*, most people are going through the hardest times of their lives. In both events, financial issues are at the core of our problems and are front and center of everyone's mind.

As stated in Principle 66 of *The Most Important Lessons in Economics and Finance*: "The public mind is generally content with feeling the universal emotion of each economic period, regardless of whether it is bad or good" (Criniti, 2014, p. 98). The essence of Hill's message is to have positive thoughts. If we have learned anything during recent times, it is equally important to not absorb the universal negative emotions that are rampant during extreme widespread adversity. This negativity is a natural reaction by the masses, but the beautiful thing is that you can choose not to adopt them. This choice can be a positive game changer for your mental and physical health.

This chapter also showed another side of Hill...an intensely scientific side. The following statements should not be taken lightly as it gives clues to how Hill thought at the deepest levels. Hill danced around the topics of education, religion, and the future while striking sharply at certain points: "The time will come when the schools and educational institutions of the country will teach the "science of prayer." Moreover, then prayer may be, and will be reduced to a science. When that time comes (it will come as soon as mankind is ready for it, and demands it), no one will approach the Universal Mind in a state of fear, for the very good reason that there will be no such emotion as fear. Ignorance, superstition, and false teaching will have disappeared, and man will have attained his true status as a child of Infinite Intelligence. A few have already attained this blessing. If you believe this prophecy is far-fetched, take a look at the human race in retrospect. Less than a hundred years ago, men believed the lightning to be evidence of the wrath of God, and feared it" (Hill, 2011, p. 299-300).

As the first proclaimed *financialist* (a term I used in *The Necessity of Finance* to label the financial scientist), I cannot dismiss the above words from Hill without some commentary. Almost one hundred years after he wrote this, it is easy to see that his words have increasingly become more accurate. The creation of the Internet became a demonstration of how this "Universal Mind" prophecy can be fulfilled. With knowledge widely disseminated, false information throughout the ages can easily be dismissed by individuals if they choose to "go there."

From *The Survival of the Richest:* "We are currently trying to squeeze through a tight bottleneck. Our prosperity has forced us to quickly solve too many serious problems. If we can emerge through these tough times though—our future may be brighter than the brightest stars in the sky. *We may find out one day that these times were just the ideal training grounds necessary to unlock our fullest potential of who we were supposed to be: the ultimate universal managers*" (Criniti, 2016, p. 453).

Science took Hill's generation out of the predicaments of the Great Depression. Science will take our generation out of the predicaments of The Great Pandemic Depression. Somewhere in this process, an increased understanding of mental and emotional intelligence by the masses will be a major determinant of the conclusion. The answers lie within our seemingly bottomless subconscious; we need to dig deep to think our way out of this box.

Bibliography

Criniti, Anthony M., IV. 2013. *The Necessity of Finance: An Overview of the Science of Management of Wealth for an Individual, a Group, or an Organization.* Philadelphia: Criniti Publishing.

Criniti, Anthony M., IV. 2014. *The Most Important Lessons in Economics and Finance: A Comprehensive Collection of Time-Tested Principles of Wealth Management.* Philadelphia: Criniti Publishing.

Criniti, Anthony M., IV. 2016. *The Survival of the Richest: An Analysis of the Relationship between the Sciences of Biology, Economics, Finance, and Survivalism.* Philadelphia: Criniti Publishing.

Hill, Napoleon. 2011. *Think and Grow Rich.* United Kingdom: Capstone Publishing Ltd.

ANTHONY M. CRINITI

About Dr. Anthony M. Criniti IV: Dr. Anthony M. Criniti IV (aka "Dr. Finance®") is the world's leading financial scientist and survivalist. A fifth-generation native of Philadelphia, Dr. Criniti is a former finance professor at several universities, a former financial planner, an active investor in diverse marketplaces, an explorer, an international keynote speaker, and has traveled around the world studying various aspects of finance.

He is an award-winning author of three #1 international bestselling finance books: *The Necessity of Finance* (2013), *The Most Important Lessons in Economics and Finance* (2014), and *The Survival of the Richest* (2016).

Dr. Criniti is also the host of the highly successful Dr. Finance® Live Podcast as well as one of the top hosts on Clubhouse. Dr. Criniti has started a grassroots movement that is changing the way that we think about economics and finance. Learn more about Doctor Finance at DrFinance.Info.

Author's Website: *www.DrFinance.info*

Book Series Website: *www.The13StepsToRiches.com*

Barry Bevier

WE GOTTA KILL THE ANTS

Our brains are the control center of our existence. In a program I completed a few years ago called The Brain Revolution with Drs. Daniel Amen and Joseph McClendon III, they liken the brain to a computer. It has hardware, the physical part of the brain, and software, the neurological or emotional part of the brain. Both parts need to function well for us to be physically and emotionally healthy.

Since Napoleon Hill wrote *Think and Grow Rich*, we have made great advances in knowledge about how the brain works and the functions of the conscious and subconscious mind.

Napoleon Hill wrote, "...the subconscious mind draws upon the forces of infinite intelligence for the power with which it voluntarily transmutes one's desires into their physical equivalent, making use always of the most practical medium by which this end may be accomplished. You can't entirely control your subconscious mind, but you can voluntarily hand over to it any plan, desire or purpose, which you wish transformed into concrete form."

"Remember your subconscious mind functions voluntarily whether you make any effort to influence it or not. This naturally suggests to you that thoughts of fear and poverty and all negative thoughts serve as stimuli in your subconscious mind unless you master these impulses and give it more desirable food upon which it may feed. The subconscious mind will not remain idle. If you fail to plant desires in your subconscious mind, it will feed upon the thoughts which reach it as the result of your neglect."

Hill describes the seven most powerful positive emotions and negative emotions. The major positive emotions are desire, faith, love, sex, enthusiasm, romance, and hope. Although there are other positive emotions, these are the seven most powerful and the ones used to create. The major negative emotions are fear, jealousy, hatred, revenge, greed, superstition, and anger.

Positive and negative emotions cannot occupy the mind at the same time —one or the other will dominate. We must make sure that we seed positive emotions so they dominate our mind. Positive thoughts are more powerful than negative thoughts and it only takes one positive thought to overcome the impact of several negative thoughts.

Our everyday lives are controlled by the power of the subconscious mind. Our conscious mind is the awareness we have in the current moment: Awareness of our surroundings, current thoughts and emotions, the physical sensations we're experiencing in our body, or whether or not we're hungry.

Our subconscious mind deals with information that's below the threshold of our current awareness: Memories, beliefs, fears, and subjective maps of reality. Our subconscious mind is very powerful and can, without our awareness, direct the course of what we do in our lives. And because of this, we must learn to choose our thoughts effectively. Because of the law of attraction, our thoughts, both conscious and subconscious, are what is creating our current reality, including our level of success in every area of our lives, be it relationships, health, career, financial or happiness.

One of my favorite sayings has become, "You don't know what you don't know." As a younger person, I did not know about the conscious and subconscious mind. Yet, looking back, the clues were all around me; I just didn't see them. Throughout my life, I've had tremendous opportunities presented to me, most of which I eagerly took advantage. Although I had a successful career and made a very comfortable living, I didn't retain the wealth that could have been associated with the level of income.

I was raised in a Christian family on a farm in Michigan. My mother had the mindset that God intended Christians and farmers to be poor (scarcity), and that wealthy people were bad (fear). Other mindsets I acquired growing up were that "Making money is not easy" and "We have to work hard to achieve success." And my favorite, "Money doesn't grow on trees." Those philosophies were imbedded in my subconscious and have had a big impact on my life.

What I've realized is that all of these opportunities allowed me to produce a good income, yet not build wealth. Because I had a scarcity mindset instilled in me from my youth, I subconsciously did not allow myself to accumulate wealth. So even though I could make money, I was unable to use it to build wealth. Does our subconscious mind work both for us and against us? It absolutely can and does.

Having grown up a farmer, it is easy to relate to Napoleon Hill's comment, "...the subconscious mind resembles a Garden Spot in which weeds will grow in abundance if the seeds of more desirable crops are not sown." In my case, my subconscious mind seeded negative thoughts about wealth, rather than me intentionally seeding my subconscious mind with thoughts of positivity, creativity, abundance and building sustainable wealth. I seeded thoughts of lack and scarcity, rather than the creation of great wealth, of which I was certainly capable.

There is so much negativity in the world today. The news networks bombard us on a daily basis with politics, wars, natural disasters, climate change, and crime. It's difficult to hear or see much of anything positive and uplifting. That's why it is so important to focus on positive thoughts.

Automatic Negative Thoughts (ANTs) come from the subconscious mind. These thoughts arise without conscious effort or intention. Some psychologists believe these are the result of negative core beliefs that are deeply embedded in our subconscious. These beliefs may have developed early in life and can influence our perceptions, attitudes, and behaviors without our conscious awareness.

Every time we have a thought, good or bad, our brain releases chemicals and an electrical signal goes across our brain, and we become aware of what we're thinking. Thoughts are real, very powerful, and they have a direct impact on how we feel and behave. They can make our mind and body feel good, or they can make us feel bad. Every cell in our body is affected by every thought we have. That's why when people get emotionally upset, they often develop physical symptoms such as headaches or stomach aches.

Once we learn about our thoughts, we can choose to think positive thoughts and feel good or choose to think negative thoughts and feel bad. We can train our thoughts to be positive and hopeful or we can allow them to be negative and upset us.

Having negative thoughts is normal, and there are two main reasons why we have them. Our prehistoric ancestors survived by constantly being on the lookout for threats, fixing problems as they arose, and then learning from their mistakes. Imagination is one of the best qualities of the human mind and we use it to imagine potential threats and problems. This enables us to solve problems before we get into trouble. Yet this capability to imagine threats can also work against us by turning our mind into a "random negative thought generator."

The second reason we may have so many automatic negative thoughts is that our negative thinking has become a habit. This is evidenced by the fact that 90% of all thoughts are repetitive; we have almost the same thoughts today that we had yesterday. If we do something often enough, including thinking negative thoughts, we create a neural pathway. The more we do it, the stronger the connections in the brain become. This is how habits get formed and why it's so hard to break a bad one.

When the ANTs are left unchecked, they steal our happiness and literally make us feel sad, depressed, and frustrated. Who likes to feel like that? Whenever we notice these ANTs, we need to crush them before they ruin our whole day.

Dr. Amen describes nine types of ANTs of which we should be aware.

1. **The All or Nothing Thinking ANT:** These thoughts happen when we make something out to be all good or all bad; there's nothing in between. We see everything in terms of black or white.

2. **The Always Thinking ANT:** This is when we think something that happened will always repeat itself. When we think in words like "always," "never," "no one," "everyone," "every time," or "everything," we're falling prey to the Always Thinking ANT.

3. **The Focusing on the Negative ANT:** This occurs when our thoughts only see the bad in a situation and ignore any of the good that might happen. I recall a recent Facebook post where a teacher did ten equations on the blackboard. Nine of the equations were correct and one was intentionally wrong. The students didn't comment on the nine correct answers. They brought up the only one wrong answer. This helped make the teacher's point that we tend to focus on the negative.

4. **The Fortune Telling ANT:** This is where we predict the worst possible outcome to a situation. For example, we just started a vacation, and the car has a flat tire. We immediately think that this is a sign everything else will go wrong on the trip.

5. **The Mind-Reading ANT:** This happens when we believe that we know what another person is thinking when they haven't even told us. Many people do this and it often gets them into trouble.

6. **The Thinking with Your Feelings ANT:** This occurs when we believe our negative feelings without ever questioning them. Feelings are very complex and sometimes lie to us. Many people believe their feelings even if there's no evidence for them.

7. **The Guilt Beatings ANT:** Guilting ourselves, or as a friend says, "Shoulding on yourself," is not a helpful emotion. In fact, guilt causes us to do things we would not normally do. Guilt beatings happen when we think with words like "should have," "must," "ought to," or "have to."

8. **The Labeling ANT:** Whenever we attach a negative label to ourselves or to someone else, we inhibit our ability to take a clearer look at the situation. Negative labels are very harmful. Some examples are labels such as stupid, nerd, jerk, idiot, or spoiled brat.

9. **The Blaming ANT:** Where we blame others for the problems in our life. Typically, we'll hear ourselves thinking, "It wasn't my fault," "That wouldn't have happened if," "How was I supposed to know?" or "It's your fault that...."

To be happy and successful in life, we will benefit from training ourselves to recognize ANTs whenever they enter our mind and squashing them. Dr. Amen has a simple technique that helps us kill the ants when they appear in our thoughts. There are five questions we can ask ourselves.

1. Ask yourself, "Is it true?" Most of the time, we will likely say yes, it is true.

2. Then ask yourself, "Is it absolutely true? Can I absolutely know that it is true? Is it true *all of the time*?" Most of the time, the answer is no.

3. Then ask yourself, "How is this thought serving me? How do I feel when I believe that thought? Does the thought make me feel sad, angry, frustrated?"

4. Finally, ask yourself, "How would I *feel* without the thought? How would I *be* without the thought?"

5. Take the original thought and completely turn it around to its opposite. Ask yourself whether this new version of the thought that is causing your suffering is not true and go through the process again.

This all takes practice, yet with repetition and time, we are able to rid ourselves of destructive ANTs. The first big step is recognizing that we have ANTs and starting to think about and question them. Being conscious of ANTs and going through the questions has helped me a lot in changing my life and manifesting my desires, and it can help you, too!

BARRY BEVIER

About Barry Bevier: Barry Bevier is a proud father of two amazing daughters, who are pursuing their passions in psychology and architecture in Southern California where he lived, worked and raised a family for over forty years. He recently moved to North Carolina to pursue the next adventure in his life's journey. Barry was raised on a family farm near Ann Arbor, Michigan. Growing up, he developed his faith in God, a strong work ethic, a love for nature, and a passion to help others. After completing his master's degree in civil engineering at the University of Michigan, he pursued a career in engineering, which eventually brought him to Southern California.

In 2000, he married the love of his life, Linda. They shared a beautiful life for ten years, until she succumbed to the effects of lupus and twenty years of treatment with prescription medications. Since then, Barry pivoted his career path into educating and helping others with their health and longevity. Barry has educated himself in alternative, natural modalities in wellness and became a Licensed Brain Health Expert through Amen Clinics. His primary focus and business is a new technology in stem cell supplementation that releases your own stem cells without invasive medical procedures.

Author's Website: *www.BRBevier.stemtech.com*

Book Series Website: *www.The13StepsToRiches.com*

Bonnie Lierse

ENERGIZER BUNNY TAPS INTO THE SUBCONSCIOUS MIND

What is ego to you? Is it good or not good? For me, I learned a lot about my ego from medium readings. That was and is a wake-up call. When my ego is working overtime, it is so fast paced—I know there is a long list of things I have to do!

So here goes: I AM MY EGO, AND IT WORKS ME DAY AND NIGHT! Sometimes, I have to tell it to stay aside, because it then gets in the way of my FOCUS!

I need my highest self to step in and help me. She has become my best friend and support team. Boy, does she have an energy and is like an energizer bunny! She and I talk all the time in my mind, with me on the outside and she on the inside! We are one in the universe and we love playing mind games together with each other.

"[The subconscious mind] alone, is the medium through which prayer maybe transmitted to the source capable of answering prayer," wrote Napoleon Hill in his book, *Think and Grow Rich*.

Did you know that the Conscious, Subconscious, and Supraconscious minds are a part of you whether you like it or not? Personally, after what I have learned from Mediumship readings with my husband, Tommy, from the afterlife, we all can be easily be influenced.

Only a small percentage maybe, five percent, use the Conscious Mind, and many individuals fail because of this.

The Subconscious Mind uses ninety five percent of your potential. Many do not know how to access that part of their mind! I am blessed I learned in a MAGICAL WAY, which I will discuss later.

The Primal Brain and the Inner Critic equals Subconscious. The highest Mind is a combination of Supraconscious and Subconscious.

So here goes: We are all in charge of our thoughts, and it delves into my creative gifts! You control your fate and you can be in control of your finances.

"Everything is energy, that all there is to it. Match the frequency of the reality you want and you cannot help but get it."
~ Albert Einstein

Your thoughts become words, your words become action, your actions become habits, your habits they become your character, your character becomes your destiny. Now that I have connection with my highest self, it is over the top extraordinary, because she knows so much more than I do or balances the weakness I may have. She is strong and powerful and an action-taker when I can be pensive and focused. I can actually hear her in my mind; she converses with me and it is powerful! Sixty-eight years young I found her, and I was smitten. I have changed a thousand percent due to this highest mind! From day to day, I have a best friend! We do share stories like buddies and it is hilarious because I truly laugh hard over this.

In hindsight, when I look back, I was the quiet, passive, sweet girl. I didn't understand the complexity of the mind then and I really did not understand ego. I thought it was confidence, and egocentric as an example. Now I understand that it is a fast-paced mind, which brings me into words. I choose carefully the words I use and you know what I mean. I never used the word, "try." I thought that to try meant that it was never going to happen, but I now know you have to at least attempt or try something for action to take place.

I took a course with Jessa Carter of "Divine Heart Dynasty" on the brain learning about the Conscious, Supraconscious, and Subconscious. It was a wake up for me that the brain is a big web of energy and emotions.

You are so curious about the small quiet voice in your mind, and from Jenna Carter's course, I've learned to hear it BIG TIME! I learned about prosperity through her sessions on the brain. It was eye opening. We never use most of our brain and we use only maybe five percent in Conscious form, but you can access the Conscious, Supraconscious, and Subconscious if you just learn to access them.

This changed my world! No one ever taps into the brain beyond the conscious, but I have been blessed to learn also from advanced training from Mediumship with my mentor and husband, Thomas B. Lierse, and my Medium, Lorri Jones! I love her to pieces and feel no competition with her on mediumship.

I am not ready to tap into anything but my highest self. She and I are so close in the mind and the heart; we laugh a lot inside my mind.

I have been writing now because of Erik Swanson, and Jon Kovach Jr., and because of them, I found some of my passions, like writing spiritual books for myself and creating children's books to publish.

"You cannot entirely control your subconscious mind, but you can voluntarily hand over it to any plan, desire or purpose which you wished transformed into concrete form."
~ Napoleon Hill

When I work in leadership, I always look for the creative energy in someone and help them reach their potential. There are many with low self-esteem, like I had most of my life, but it's worth taking a new turn and journey to change that forever. Many of the young or mature people I work with may not understand that they can overcome their low self-esteem but if I can tap into something in them, I am fulfilled. When I had a decorating business, I would help bring out the team's best energy that they didn't know they had.

Wherever I go, I can get a big smirk or smile out of people because they are elated someone has heartstrings and cares.

I use to work at a dating service that was old school with index cards. We had all the information on the individuals and we would match them up by their specific personalities and details. Sometimes I had to tap into their subconscious mind to read their needs.

It was such a privilege to do that successfully and I actually love working with people anywhere.

When you tap into your Subconscious Mind, you are in for a journey that is unexplainable and you have NO idea what you are in for! Actually, you are not in for a ride, you are in for a change of the Subconscious Mind. ARE YOU READY?

"You have not had time to master faith. Be Patient. Be Persistent."
~ Napoleon Hill

BONNIE LIERSE

About Bonnie Lierse: Bonnie Zaruches Lierse is extremely artistic and creative, with an entrepreneurial bent. Besides that, she is a seasoned agent with more than twenty years' experience in real estate in the New York/Long Island area. She relocated to Northern Virginia in 2012 and continued her real estate career there.

Another passion of hers is creating leaders by working in business leadership development with *Leadership Team Development (LTD)*, and marketing products supplied by Amway. She was also a member of *The Screen Cartoonist Guild of Motion Pictures* for many years. Also, she did freelanced for *Sesame Street* in New York City. In addition, she was a District Director for an interior accessory design company, as her own business.

Bonnie is blessed with five beautiful grandchildren and is very close with her children and family, some of whom are also in Virginia. Her missions are leadership, mentorship, paying it forward, and changing lives one at a time. Her motto is *"You be the difference!"*

Author's Website: *www.amway.com/myshop/SplashFXEnterprises*

Book Series Website: *www.The13StepsToRiches.com*

Brian Schulman

IS YOUR SUBCONSCIOUS MIND PRIMED FOR SUCCESS? MASTER YOUR MIND

"Let's call this meeting to order. Alright people, what's the good news? Annie, my content expert, where are you on creating the content of our latest mastermind?"

"Everything's right on track and looks great! You've really outdone yourself with this one."

"Andrew, my marketing guru, how are we doing with generating a name for the mastermind?"

"It's spot on! All the focus groups consistently choose the same one."

"Great. Where are we on marketing and branding?"

"Everyone's loving it. We're getting overwhelmingly positive feedback on the designs."

"Jonathan, my rockstar web designer, how's that landing page going?"

"Dude, this landing page is going to slay."

"Jean Carlos, registration and payment?"

"Smooth as a baby's bottom."

"Bobbie, my email marketing and copy guru, what's the latest with the email list and our campaigns?"

"Ready when you are boss!"

"Outstanding."

"Syma, are we ready to give away our give-away?"

"Yes. And it is AWESOME! I remember loving the giveaway I got when I was in the mastermind!"

"Annie, I'm loving the twelve-month content calendar you created to always keep us top of mind. Team, this is going to be our most successful mastermind yet—and it's because of each of you."

"Excuse me, Brian, you just had a call from Linkedin. They want you to be their international ambassador for LinkedIn Video and livestreaming, to teach others how to build community on the platform. What do you want me to tell them?"

"Please, set up a Zoom so we can talk about it face to face."

"Brian, don't forget on Tuesday you have the interview with Oprah for the cover story on the 'LinkedIn Made Easy Mastermind: Behind The Scenes Exclusive Ways To Leverage LinkedIn As Podcasters.'"

"Thank you, Nancy."

"The launch-party event in Florida. Does anyone on the team still need swag and do we have our swag giveaways ready? Did you guys see the badges for the networking event? THEY. ARE. PHEN-OMENAL! Yes, Talisha, I called Matt at Ticket Time Machine to let him know we received them and that we couldn't be happier. Have all the VIPs been assigned a point-person? Let's have those point-people make a touchpoint and reach out this week."

"We got you covered. It is all taken care of!"

"Thank you! Nancy, any final thoughts before we break?"

"We are perfectly on schedule and ready to launch on time! We are moving ahead with an all-virtual format with ten people participating in each six-week Cohort. We don't want this to get so large that people feel nameless and faceless. The self-assessment for the participants was given a 'go' by everyone, so that's checked off the list. The slide deck for each session is complete. The agenda for each session was added where it was needed and post session action items are DONE! You guys rock!"

"Thanks, Nancy. I gotta tell you all, YOU guys are the reason this is happening! I deeply appreciate you and all the time and effort you put in every day. This is it! It is go time, people!"

"I designed this mastermind specifically for Podcasters. We are going to gather and help so many people exceed their goals!"

"Annie, Andrew, Bobbie and Jean Carlos—the way you all streamlined the process is a thing of beauty! And Jonathan, the rework on the website is brilliant. Syma, way to take the ball and run with it! The design for the giveaway is better than I pictured it! Nancy, thank you for being my brain and voice. It helps more than you know."

"Finally, Happy Taco Tuesday! Lunch is on me! The taco truck will be downstairs in approximately ten minutes. Enjoy!"

When planning a mastermind, your mental board of advisors should consist of individuals who have experience in group facilitation, organization, and the specific area of focus for the group.
Potential advisors could include:

- A facilitator or group coach with experience in leading and organizing successful masterminds. They could advise you on how to structure meetings, create an effective agenda, and manage group dynamics.

- Experts in the area of focus for the group. For example, if the group's focus is on business development, you may want to include advisors with experience in entrepreneurship, marketing, and finance. They could advise you on specific topics to cover during meetings and offer valuable insights and advice to group members.

- Individuals who have successfully participated in a mastermind in the past. They could provide you with valuable insights on what worked well and what didn't work well in their experience, and help you avoid common pitfalls.

Some things they could tell you:

- How to structure the meetings and create an effective agenda that keeps the group engaged and on track.

- How to manage group dynamics and keep the group focused on its goals.

- Tips for selecting group members and keeping the group size manageable.

- How to measure progress and success for the group.

- How to keep the group motivated and engaged over time.

It's important to note that a mastermind is a collaborative effort and the success of the group depends on the active participation and commitment of all members.

Welcome to my internally visualized board meeting with my team of advisors.

For three months, I had this meeting every day. It was the first order of business and it was a group ritual. Every person on the team had their own meeting where they visualized success!

Together, we were transmuting that vision into a reality. I was developing a new mastermind with my team and I was making sure my subconscious mind was a productive member of the team!

Whether you want it to or not, the subconscious mind is always alert and working. When you are sleeping and your alarm goes off or there is noise in the house, that's a good thing. However, if you are not aware, and mindful, of what you are feeding your subconscious mind, you are very likely watering the wrong seeds. But it is possible to plant any plan, thought, or purpose in your subconscious mind in order to transmute them and manifest them into being!

Can you control your subconscious mind? Not entirely. Nonetheless, you can consciously choose which seeds you provide to your brain for planting through the power of autosuggestion. How?

The "invisible counselor technique" was developed by Napoleon Hill to access the subconscious mind when seeking advice and it is one of the best ways to reprogram your subconscious mind.

It takes commitment to obstinately continue a course of action despite difficulty or opposition to influence your subconscious. It takes special attention to emotions. You need to fill your mind with positive emotions and reject the negative ones. If you are filled with fear, failure, anger, jealousy, greed, revenge, etc. that is what the subconscious mind will cultivate.

Our brain more deeply encodes negative than positive. It is a built in "survival mechanism," therefore, one negative thought can drown out all the positive thoughts and feelings. Every time my visualized team met, there were only positive things to share, everything was running smoothly and on time. If something arose, we efficiently, effectively, and easily resolved it.

After visualizing every detail of those meetings in my head for three months, I successfully launched another mastermind, *LinkedIn Made Easy Mastermind: Behind The Scenes Exclusive Ways To Leverage LinkedIn As Podcasters,* and it has been a great success multiple times over. Yes, I worked with a "real" team to create the superior product I provide to participants and make it to launch.

If I had allowed my subconscious mind to wander in doubt and fear, I never would have made it to launch. Solidifying my intention every day by holding those mental meetings, I was telling my brain which seeds to water.

What makes you successful? Your *faith* in yourself. Your *desire* to see it through. Your *organized planning*. Your *persistence*. Your ability to reprogram your *subconscious mind* such that failure is not an option.

We are always planting seeds for our subconscious mind whether we realize it. Whether it is picturing in your head where you parked so you can find your car in a parking lot, seeing yourself rocking the big presentation you are going to give, imagining introducing yourself to someone new and even when you visualize in your head all the ways you are going to fail, your subconscious mind waters those seeds every time you do it! Which is why the very second a negative thought or emotion enters your head, you must replace it with a positive thought.

LinkedIn Made Easy Mastermind: Behind The Scenes Exclusive Ways To Leverage LinkedIn As Podcasters is the result of consciously controlling the flow of information to my subconscious mind so that my visualizations took a "physical" form. It is the secret to success for all of us!

BRIAN SCHULMAN

About Brian Schulman: Known as the Godfather and Pioneer, of LinkedIn Video and one of the world's premiere live streaming and video marketing experts, using a heart-centered, growth mindset while leveraging the power of LinkedIn's community and platform, Brian has transformed how business is conducted on LinkedIn worldwide. Founder and CEO of VoiceYourVibe, Brian brings his twenty-plus years experience, wealth of knowledge and proven Digital Marketing expertise, to Podcasters, Entrepreneurs, C-Suite Executives globally as an advisor and mentor through groundbreaking Masterminds, Workshops, 1-on-1 and Team Mastery Coaching. Brian and Team work with clients strategically to build and increase strong brand recognition, grow your network, generate consistent, reliable revenue streams, and create a purpose-driven message that sets you apart from the 1 billion business professionals on LinkedIn.

10X #1 Bestselling Author and internationally known Keynote Speaker, Brian's expertise, insights and two Global Award-Winning LIVE Shows have been featured on NASDAQ, Forbes, Thrive Global, Yahoo Finance, Viacom, ROKU TV, The CW, multiple #1 best-selling books, syndicated on Smart TV Networks and hundreds of shows and podcasts, reaching millions worldwide. Among his many awards and honors, Brian has been named a "2X LinkedIn Top Voice," "LinkedIn Video Creator Of The Year," 3X "Top 50 Most Impactful People of LinkedIn," and 2X "LinkedIn Global Leader of The Year." His two global award-winning weekly LIVE shows #ShoutOutSaturday and #WhatsGoodWednesday, broadcasted in 120+ countries, were named "Best LIVE Festive Show of The Year" at the IBM TV Awards.

Author's Website: *www.VoiceYourVibe.com*

Book Series Website: *www.The13StepsToRiches.com*

Candace & David Rose

POSITIVE VS. NEGATIVE

*"Positive and negative emotions cannot occupy the mind at the same time.
ONE OR THE OTHER MUST DOMINATE."*
~ Napoleon Hill

CANDACE & DAVID ROSE

About Candace & David Rose: Candace & David are #1 Bestselling Authors in the book series, *The 13 Steps to Riches*. Candace and David grew up together and currently live in Alvarado, Texas. They both are veterans of the US Army. David served as a mechanic, and Candace as a Legal NCO.

David is currently a Product Release Specialist, delivering Liquid Oxygen and Nitrogen to various manufacturing plants and hospitals throughout Texas. Candace specializes in helping people organize their space, both physically and mentally—with the ultimate goal of helping you change your box and find more joy in your life.

Author's Website: *www.ChangeYourBox.com*

Book Series Website: *www.The13StepsToRiches.com*

Corey Poirier

MANIFESTING THE MIND

Before my twenties, I never even thought of my subconscious mind as a thing. I certainly didn't feel I had any control over it. I simply saw it, at most, as something that was working in the background, whether I liked it or not.

I sure didn't think my thoughts on a conscious level could have any impact on it. Over time, I recognized the error of my ways.

When it really happened, I discovered my purpose.

As I slowly discovered my calling, I noticed I began to speak kinder words to myself, and as I did that, I noticed that my subconscious mind went to work in creating a world that matched my new attitude.

Instead of being hard, things became easier. Instead of me almost dreading waking up, I got excited to start each day. Instead of me dreading my job, I started to be grateful for it.

The reason I know this was happening on a subconscious level is I wasn't even aware that it was happening and honestly didn't even notice that I was practicing positive self-talk. Interestingly, regardless of whether I was aware of it or not, it was still happening.

Ah, the power of the subconscious mind.

Once I clued into what was happening, which was after I read *Think and Grow Rich* by the way, I began to start programming, in a sense, my subconscious mind.

What we might call miracles, or at least magic, started to happen. I started to experience things in weeks which once took months or even years.

I tapped into manifestation and began manifesting things like my first TEDx Talk, bestselling books, a comedy gig at the famed Second City, a Rock Recording of the Year nominated Album, interviews with the likes of Jack Canfield and Lisa Nichols, stages with the likes of Deepak Chopra... and even my ideal girlfriend—who I'm still with, and have two kids with, eight years later.

I even manifested a business relationship with one of the world's bestselling authors and we are currently working on a documentary around his work.

All of this, some of it intentionally, some of it not, I don't believe would have been possible had I not started tapping into the power of the subconscious mind.

Now, I won't pretend to know how it all works; I just know it does.

One thing I know is that if you don't actively and intentionally program your subconscious mind, it will be programmed by your thoughts just the same.

If you put negative in, that is likely what you'll draw and attract more of. If you put positive in, that is what you'll likely draw and attract more of. So, what do you want more of?

Before I started leveraging the power of my subconscious mind, my thoughts weren't serving me well. Once I did, everything changed.

Now that I've told you a bit about how the subconscious mind changed my life, let me share a bit about how I started programming it.

First, I started journaling. I felt that if I was writing it down, my subconscious mind was looking at it, too.

Next, I created a very personalized vision board—I figured if I was seeing it, my subconscious mind was watching.

And then I did affirmations. I figured if I was saying it, my subconscious mind was listening.

The hardest one of these for me was affirmations. I thought they were kind of cheesy. The reason?

I recalled when Al Franken had his character, Stuart Smalley, on Saturday Night Live. The character did affirmations, and he would look himself in the mirror and say to himself, "I'm good enough, I'm smart enough, and doggone it, people like me!"

I cringed every time he said it and laughed hysterically at the absurdity of it all.

Since my subconscious mind had been watching me laugh and cringe at his sayings (his affirmations), it truly impacted my ability to say affirmations myself without also judging myself.

So, I encouraged (forced?) myself to do them anyway "just to see what may happen," and low and behold, I saw results.

Eventually, I created new programming around my take on affirmations, and my subconscious mind ultimately ended up being, as Neville Goddard might say, "At my command."

As I close off this chapter, I simply want to say that if you're reading this book but haven't read *Think and Grow Rich* yet—you need to run and grab it right now. It will introduce you to the power of your subconscious mind and may even give you the tools to leverage it as well. For certain, it will open up your mind to what is truly possible.

Whether it teaches you how to leverage the power of your subconscious mind, which it has done for me, or just opens you up to the idea that there may be a power there you haven't been using knowingly—simply opening up to it being a possible game changer for you is half the battle, and *Think and Grow Rich* will likely help you with that part.

Until then, my friends, here's to your greater success.

Corey

Facebook: *www.facebook.com/corey.poirier.1/*
LinkedIn: *www.linkedin.com/in/speakercoreypoirier/*
Instagram: *www.instagram.com/thatspeakerguy*
Email: *BluTalksBrand@gmail.com*

COREY POIRIER

About Corey Poirier: Corey Poirier is a multiple-time TEDx Speaker. He is also the host of the top-rated "Let's Do Influencing" Radio Show, founder of the growing bLU Talks brand, and has been featured in multiple television specials. He is also a Barnes and Noble, Amazon, Apple Books, and Kobo Bestselling Author, Award Winning Author, and the co-author of the Wall Street Journal / USA Today Bestseller, Quitless.

A columnist with Entrepreneur and Forbes magazine, he has been featured in/on various mediums and is one of the few leaders featured twice on the popular Entrepreneur on Fire show.

He has also interviewed over 6,500 of the world's top leaders, and he has spoken on-site at Harvard and Columbia University, and more recently to Microsoft team leaders and at Inner Circles, which have featured everyone from Brian Tracy to Mark Victor Hansen to Phil Collen (Def Leppard).

Also appearing on the popular Evan Carmichael YouTube Channel, he is a New Media Summit Icon of Influence, was recently listed as the #5 Influencer in Entrepreneurship by Thinkers 360, and listed on the 2021 Brainz CREA Global Awards as an honouree, and he is a Humanitarian Hero Award Nominee, Entrepreneur of the Year Nominee, Champion Award (Business from The Heart) nominee, and to demonstrate his versatility, a Rock Recording of the Year Nominee who has performed stand-up comedy more than 700 times, including an appearance at the famed Second City.

Author's Website: *www.ThatSpeakerGuy.com*

Book Series Website: *www.The13StepsToRiches.com*

Deb Scott

FIELD OF CONSCIOUSNESS

"THE SUBCONSCIOUS MIND consists of a field of consciousness in which every impulse of thought or sensation that reaches the objective mind through any of the five senses is classified and recorded, and from which thoughts may be recalled or withdrawn as letters may be taken from a filing cabinet."
~ Napoleon Hill

DEB SCOTT

About Deb Scott: Deb Scott, BA, CPC, and Realtor, was a high honors biology major at Regis College in Weston, Massachusetts, and spent over two decades as an award-winning cardio-thoracic sales specialist in the New England area. She is a best-selling author of T*he Sky is Green & The Grass is Blue: Turning Your Upside Down World Right Side Up.* She is an award-winning podcaster of *The Best People We Know Show.*

Following in her family's footsteps, she is a third-generation Realtor in Venice, Florida. As a certified life coach, Deb speaks and teaches how to turn bad situations into positive, successful results. As a top sales specialist, she enjoys teaching people "sales without selling," believing that integrity, good communication, and respect are the winning equation to all outstanding success and happiness in life.

Author's Website: *www.DebScott.com*

Book Series Website: *www.The13StepsToRiches.com*

Dori Ray

DOMINATING DESIRES & EMOTIONAL FEELING

"The subconscious mind receives and files sense impressions or thoughts regardless of their nature. You may VOLUNTARILY plant in your subconscious mind any plan, thought, or purpose which you desire to translate into its physical or monetary equivalent. The subconscious acts first on the dominating desires which have been mixed with emotional feeling, such as FAITH."
~ Napoleon Hill

DORI RAY

About Dori Ray: Dori "On Purpose" Ray is a native Philadelphian. As a businesswoman, her mission is to help people transform their minds, bodies, and bank accounts! Dori was educated in the Philadelphia Public School System. She graduated from the Philadelphia High School for Girls in 1982 and Howard University School of Business in 1986 with a BBA in Marketing. Dori is a Delta Sigma Pi Business Fraternity and Delta Sigma Theta Sorority, Inc. member.

Dori leads teams around the world. She is a sought-after speaker and trainer in her industry and beyond. She is an experienced Re-Entry Coach who has helped hundreds of Returning Citizens get back on track after incarceration.

Having suffered from depression for twenty years, she always reaches back to share her story and help break the cycle of silence. Her audience loves her authenticity! Book Dori for speaking engagements with her information below.

Author's Website: *www.linktr.ee/DoriOnPurpose*

Book Series Website: *www.The13StepsToRiches.com*

Elaine R. Sugimura

THE HIGHEST POSSIBILITY: THRIVER-SHIP

Creating riches requires us to have the desire to cause and create whatever is possible in our lives. The important question I ask myself is, "What is the key to shaping my desires so that this occurs?" Napoleon Hill teaches us that our subconscious mind is where every idea and thought is recorded and can be recalled later. To achieve what we desire, one must be open to the possibilities available to them by choosing and positioning their plan/strategy into their subconscious mind. This is what is ultimately needed to achieve anything and everything we desire in our lives. Sounds simple, right?

Let's go back in our memory bank and think about the many days and nights that our subconscious mind is working for or against us. It works even when we are sleeping. It conditions our desires, habits, and actions. So, if we can embed success into our subconscious mind, wouldn't it be true that faith, creativity, and belief allow us to achieve the plan/strategy we set forth?

I have found several ways to overcome my victim and survivor mentality. Daily, I choose to plant the desire into my subconscious by practicing both meditation and visualization. If I know what I desire and have a vision of how to achieve it, I allow my subconscious mind to take me to that place of WIN/WIN. For example, if I say I want to cross off a major item on my life's bucket list, I immediately imagine what it will take from me to cause and create this desire and make it a reality.

For so many years, I only dreamt about the possibility of retiring, and it is now here. I never fully visualized what retirement would look like as I was just a "human doing" versus a "human being" most of my adult life. I've learned that patience and persistence are required when dealing with our subconscious, as negative and undesirable thoughts are not part of the success equation. I am now understanding that when I place those positive thoughts in front of me and plant the seeds in my subconscious mind, manifesting what I desire— it happens! I am currently making the biggest move of my life, and I'm not clear on where I am going, but this journey is both exciting and daunting.

Emotions are our natural instinctive state of mind as we allow them into our subconscious mind. There are seven key positive and negative emotions that we can also refer to as ways of being. Consistently, the negative emotions get introduced regardless of how we want to control them; however, from Napoleon Hill's teachings, we know that positive emotions are introduced via auto-suggestion.

Hill refers to the subconscious as the "inner audience." In other words, the result of what we create is based on how we deal with and allow information that is being absorbed into our subconscious mind. Therefore, our inner audience takes note and reacts accordingly. So, I come back to this question, "What is it that we are willing to shift when it comes to our victim and survivor stories?" There is a thriver in each of us—so what will it take to create that each day of our lives?

A great exercise I learned in an advanced transformational leadership program is that we must learn to "hear" what our "heart" is desiring. Thus, through auto-suggestion and positive emotions, we can speak the language that our subconscious can understand—otherwise, it will not "hear" our calls. Thus, the language our inner audience truly understands is that of our emotions. Let's explore the seven positive and negative emotions below:

The Seven Positive Emotions are: Desire, faith, love, intimacy, passion, joy, and hope. Of course, there are many others, but these are the major emotions that are required to cause and create what you desire.

The Seven Negative Emotions are: Fear, jealousy, anger, scarcity, pain, doubt, and worthlessness.

What is clear to me is that both positive and negative emotions cannot occupy the mind at the same time. Typically, one type of emotion dominates over the other. It is up to us to be responsible by ensuring our minds absorb every positive emotion we are conjuring up. The only way a thriver creates this is by creating positive habits. Our negative thoughts can be referred to as "a racket." I learned that a racket is when we consistently allow the negative emotions to overrule our positive habits/ actions. Think about it. How many times have you achieved the same result because you consistently behave and respond the same exact way you did during a prior incident? How you do anything is how you do everything.

Another good example of this is when we turn to spirituality or prayer when all else fails. If you pray with the emotions of fear and doubt, your prayers are futile. Thus, praying is an art and deep science is involved behind it. Prayer is a ray of hope for people in times of hardship. You see, prayer is deeply connected to your subconscious mind. Our subconscious mind is the inner audience that can affect our behavior without realizing it.

For example, have you ever had that moment when you met someone for the first time, and you felt an instantaneous connection? This is the direct response from your subconscious mind, and it plays a key role in attracting things in and out of your life. It is important to note that the subconscious mind understands visuals and not words. This means that you should visualize that you have already received what it is you desire whether it is through prayer or any other means in your life. Living with the Thriver-ship mentality allows you to constantly visualize a positive state of mind. Nothing will become your reality until you accept it. Remember the following:

• Before your prayer reaches infinite intelligence, it moves from an original state of vibration to a spiritual one. Faith is the only emotion that can transform into spiritual form. Faith and fear are not emotions that can coexist in one's mind.

• Your subconscious mind does not reason, it does not analyze or think. Our subconscious does what it is trained to do by its master—that is YOU and ME.

Here are two quotes that embody what I am sharing with you:

"Good or Bad you will always reap what you sow... You will always harvest the consequences of your choices."
~ Randy Alcorn

"If you don't like what you are reaping, you had better change what you have been sowing."
~ Jim Rohn

What are you "hearing" from these two quotes? These two examples clearly demonstrate the importance of thinking positively, planting the right thoughts, and noting that the consequence of any negative thoughts will be the result of whatever choice you make.

You see, our thoughts and actions are memorized and stored, so we tend to always choose what is comfortable. If we choose to stay in our comfort zone, challenges will surface. If we keep doing the same things and believing the same thoughts, will we get a different result? The answer to that question is no. In business, we always say, garbage in = garbage out. Thus, if we keep doing things in the same manner, it only solidifies and reinforces what does not serve us, as the result never changes.

If you stay in that space of comfort, eventually, your world of possibilities gets smaller and smaller as your comfort zone will only grow, and your result will be the strengthening of your historical beliefs and patterns. This is the Victim and Survivor mentality. Thus, if we challenge ourselves to be uncomfortable, the possibilities of what we can create with positive thinking and emotions are endless.

As key transformational trainers share in their teachings, "Be the uncontested author of your LIFE, not the critic of your life." Know who is boss by planting the positive seeds and know there is a way to flip the auto-pilot switch (your subconscious mind) to the ON position. Our subconscious mind is always working for you, morning, noon, and night so you can achieve all you set out to achieve. What has been so inspiring to me is how I have been able to learn how to create the tools and learn the techniques to ensure I am nurturing my mind in an urgent and rigorous way.

If it is to BE, it is up to ME! This is a mantra I live by after learning how to master my subconscious mind. As a results-oriented person who loves competition, I want results now versus later, so leaning in and challenging myself to take risks, turning each obstacle into an opportunity, and speaking with clarity supports my ability to keep my mind in a positive emotional thinking state. I am continually repeating this pattern to ensure my choices are equivalent to what I desire. This, my friends, equals a WIN/WIN!

In closing, I want to share a powerful thriver-ship tool that works for me when it comes to shifting my subconscious thinking patterns. Stretch yourself to shift what is not working. Implement those shifts both strategically and habitually and they will then become your personality!

"You are the sum total of your dominating most prominent thoughts."
~ Napolean Hill

ELAINE SUGIMURA

About Elaine R. Sugimura: Elaine is an accomplished CEO turned Business Consultant and Life Strategist who has a passion for creating Leaders amongst Leaders. With over thirty-five-plus years in the fashion and food and beverage industry, she has a passion for not only leading but also supporting those who are seeking to reinvent who they are no matter where they are in life. She is a two-time breast cancer survivor, and she knows a thing or two about surviving and thriving.

Fun fact: she is an adrenaline junkie—the higher, the faster, the better. Her love for adventure has led her to travel to many parts of the world by plane, train, and automobile. She and her husband, Hiro, share their home in Northern California. They have raised two extraordinary sons, Bryce and Cole, and have added two beautiful daughters-in-law, Erica and Giselle, to their growing family. Her legacy is to share what is possible when we open ourselves up to the issues that hold us back. Her Life's mission is to move those who are just surviving into Thrivers!

Author's Website: *www.ElaineRSugimura.com*

Book Series Website: *www.The13StepstoRiches.com*

Elizabeth Anne Walker

LIFE'S KEY

Napoleon Hill referred to it as the connecting link and I refer to it as the key: The subconscious mind is what unlocks our greatest potential in life! Without its support, it is unlikely that we will achieve anything that goes against our current status quo. How do we get its support if we don't even know what it is?

Let's explore a little more about the subconscious mind so that we can make sense of how it works and how we can apply it to reaching our potential. The following are the qualities or prime directives of the subconscious mind:

1. **Stores Our Memories:** The subconscious mind provides the coordination for the storage of memories. In 1957, the Penfield Study probed an older woman's brain, and she remembered everything from a party when she was five. In 1960, Carl Pribram won a Nobel Prize when he postulated that memories were stored both in the subconscious mind as well as the cells of the body. The body processes the body's memory via the subconscious mind.

2. **Organizes All Our Memories:** The subconscious mind organizes all the memories which are stored in the nervous system. This was first postulated by Sigmund Freud in 1899 and agreed upon ever since. The way it organizes these memories is that it uses "indexes" to point to the stored memories and to allow you to access these memories.

3. **The Domain of Our Emotions:** The subconscious mind is the domain of the emotions. Even though they are often felt

consciously, emotions are not the domain of the conscious mind. They are generated by, maintained by, and are the responsibility of the subconscious mind. In 1924, Sigmund Freud discovered this and further research by R. Lang in 2004 confirmed it.

4. **Represses Memories with Unresolved Negative Emotions:** The subconscious mind is also charged with the responsibility of repressing memories with unresolved negative emotion. The memory will be repressed with the emotion intact until it can be resolved. Frederickson 1992 evidenced this in her works on recovery from sexual abuse. The repressed negative emotions are trapped in the body, and in many cases can cause blockages to the flow of communication through the neural network pathways of the body.

5. **Present Repressed Memories to Release the Emotions:** Memories which have been repressed are then presented to release the trapped negative emotions. At the time of presentation of the memory, releasing the emotions by "rationalizing" the memory can clear the negative emotions from mind and body.

6. **Keep Repressed Emotions Repressed for Protection:** The subconscious mind also has the option of keeping the memories repressed.

7. **Runs the Body:** We do not require the conscious mind to beat our heart or expand our lungs to breathe, as our subconscious mind does these for us.

8. **Preserves the Body:** The subconscious mind is also in charge of preserving the body. In times of extreme danger, many people notice that the subconscious mind takes over, and the conscious mind is not at all involved at that moment.

9. **A Highly Moral Being:** The subconscious mind will enforce any morality which it has been taught and has come to believe is true. This is important in healing.

10. **Takes Directions, Follows Orders:** The subconscious mind likes to have direction from the conscious mind.

11. **Controls & Maintains All Perceptions:** As our sensory perceptions come into the neurology from outside the body, they must

pass through the subconscious mind before they become available as conscious perceptions.

12. **Generates, Stores, Distributes, & Transmits Energy:** As the "manager" of the body, the subconscious mind also oversees the energy of the body. Most of the energy in the body is generated by the interaction of glucose with oxygen.

13. **Responds with Instinct & Habit:** Some instincts are built-in at birth, such as the Fight or Flight response. Habits are cultivated over time.

14. **Needs Repetition-Building Habits:** When cultivating a habit, it is a good idea to repeat it often until it is taken over by the subconscious mind.

15. **Continually Seeks More & More:** The subconscious mind is directed to continually seek more and more.

16. **Is a Whole Integrated Functioning Unit.**

17. **Is Symbolic:** The subconscious mind is symbolic. It is, in many areas, pre-literate, so it creates and uses, and responds to symbols (thank you Carl Jung for first pointing this out to us).

18. **Works on the Principle of Least Effort:** The subconscious mind works on the principle of least effort, and that means it will do as little as it can get away with.

19. **Takes Everything Personally:** The saying in psychology is, "Perception is projection." What you see is who you are. So, think the best about everybody you meet.

20. **Cannot Process a Negative:** Finally, and we have already discussed this earlier, make sure you are telling your subconscious mind what to do, think, and be—as opposed to telling it what not to do, think, and be.

I once spent a lot of time conditioning my own subconscious mind in a way that was in direct conflict with what I truly wanted. I had been very sick for a long time with five autoimmune disorders. One was extremely rare at the time, *Lichen Planus Vulvaris*, where the mucous membranes on all my nether regions as well as my mouth, nose and eyes would eat each themselves to the point of ulceration with no skin remaining. I had forty-seven operations in a three-year period and was in a wheelchair, unable to walk after an accident in surgery where my femoral nerve was severed.

I kept telling myself I was hopeless—if only I didn't have these issues, if only I had never been abused I wouldn't have held all this negativity in my body. I blamed my life, the medical system and anyone else I could for my lack of health. I got sicker and sicker to the point where I felt my only way out was to die.

A friend of mine had a spare ticket to an event and begrudgingly I bought it. I was convinced nothing would work and because of this my subconscious mind made it so. I went to the event in my wheelchair, unable to walk and only able to stand barely long enough to go to the toilet. The event started and the subconscious mind was discussed in detail. We did meditations and letting go exercises and got excited about all that we could learn in terms of how to be in charge of our subconscious mind.

That first night, the discussions culminated in a fire walk. As they wheeled me out, I assumed that I was going to watch. Low and behold, they wheeled me up to the fire lane, helped me to stand and then I was asked to "Make my Move," a chant type action we had learned earlier in the day. I did it and then walked across the fire! I not only walked—I walked across fire! I had done it! I literally left my wheelchair at that event and never went back in it again!

The next week my specialist said to me, "This is impossible!" as I walked into her office. I told her that if she was going to program my mind with that kind of attitude I was out! She asked me to wait and did some tests and declared it a miracle. I told her it was the power of the subconscious mind. I cancelled my next appointment and have been walking ever since.

I am so grateful for what I've learned in this area. I went on to study the subconscious mind and now teach people all over the world about it so they, too, can move forward in their lives.

ELIZABETH ANNE WALKER

About Elizabeth Walker: Elizabeth is Australia's leading Female Integrated NLP Trainer, an international speaker with Real Success, and the host of Success Resources's (Australia's largest and most successful events promoter, including speakers such as Tony Robbins and Sir Richard Branson) inaugural Australian Women's Program "The Seed." Elizabeth has guided many people to achieve complete personal breakthroughs and phenomenal personal and business growth. With over twenty-five years of experience transforming the lives of hundreds of thousands of people, Elizabeth's goal is to assist leaders to create the reality they choose to live, impacting millions on a global scale.

A thought leader who has worked alongside people like Gary Vaynerchuck, Kerwin Rae, Jeffery Slayter, and Kate Gray, Elizabeth has an outstanding method of delivering heart with business.

As a former lecturer in medicine at the University of Sydney and lecturer in nursing at Western Sydney University, Elizabeth was instrumental in the research and development of the stillbirth and neonatal death pathways, ensuring each family in Australia went home knowing what happened to their child, and felt understood, heard, and seen.

A former Australian Champion in Trampolining and Australian Dance sport, Elizabeth has always been passionate about the mindset and skills required to create the results you are seeking.

Author's Website: *www.ElizabethAnneWalker.com*

Book Series Website: *www.The13StepsToRiches.com*

Erin Ley

DOMINATING INFLUENCE

Napoleon Hill brilliantly states in his classic book from 1937, *Think and Grow Rich,* "The subconscious mind consists of a field of consciousness, in which every impulse of thought that reaches the objective mind through any of the five senses is classified and recorded, and from which thoughts may be recalled or withdrawn as letters may be taken from a filing cabinet."

The subconscious mind is fascinating! Every human walking the planet runs ninety-five percent of their day based on what they've programmed into their subconscious mind. From birth to age eight, we take on the beliefs of our family, teachers, friends, church—anyone and everyone we trust. We take on their beliefs and make them our own. We then go a whole lifetime living that program out—until we become aware that many of those beliefs we hold in our subconscious are no longer serving us.

Many people go a lifetime believing they're doomed to a life of suffering because that was what their ancestors experienced. Others develop the habit of negative self-talk, which creates a self-imposed prison inside their own mind.

These limiting beliefs and the self-doubt—such as feeling unworthy, not good enough, not smart enough, and so on—can lead to low self-esteem and lack of self-confidence. Once you recognize their hold on you and begin to realize they're not true, you can reprogram your subconscious.

Awareness is huge. Awareness is the key to unlocking and unpacking all the stored beliefs in your subconscious mind that are no longer serving you and replacing them with positive, empowering beliefs that will serve you so that you can begin to live your best life.

In *Think and Grow Rich*, Napoleon Hill said, "Let us therefore describe here the seven major positive emotions, so that you may draw upon the positives, and avoid the negatives, when giving instructions to your subconscious mind."

THE SEVEN MAJOR POSITIVE EMOTIONS:

- The emotion of DESIRE
- The emotion of FAITH
- The emotion of LOVE
- The emotion of SEX
- The emotion of ENTHUSIASM
- The emotion of ROMANCE
- The emotion of HOPE

THE SEVEN NEGATIVE EMOTIONS:

- The emotion of FEAR
- The emotion of JEALOUSY
- The emotion of HATRED
- The emotion of REVENGE
- The emotion of GREED
- The emotion of SUPERSTITION
- The emotion of ANGER

Positive and negative emotions cannot occupy the mind at the same time. One or the other must be dominant. It is your responsibility to make sure that positive emotions constitute the dominating influence of your mind. Here, the law of habit will come to your aid. Form the habit of applying and using the positive emotions. Eventually, they will dominate your mind so completely that the negatives cannot enter it.

When I was going through a shocking and tumultuous divorce from 2014-2016, after being with my ex-husband for twenty-two years, thinking we were like Mickey and Minnie Mouse, I allowed the negative thinking to take over. I was the only one in the position to allow that, and it derailed my life more than divorce did.

The more concerned I became with my financials, the more problematic the financials became. The more I second-guessed my maternal skills, the more my maternal skills became compromised. The more confused and fearful of my future I was, the bleaker my future became—until I did what I did when I was diagnosed with non-Hodgkins lymphoblastic lymphoma. At that time, in 1991, my identity became questionable; my future was thrown in the air, and I knew I had to reclaim my right to life. I knew I had to become fully aligned with who I truly am physically, mentally, and spiritually. I began to implement what I learned in 1991 as I went through the divorce process.

After learning about meditation, visualization, affirmations, and so much more, I began to slide into the driver's seat of my own life, as opposed to life driving me. It was incredibly freeing. At that time, others' opinions of me became irrelevant. I became comfortable within my own skin. Life went from being difficult to being as if I was riding a magic carpet. Let me explain.

In 1991, I learned about "flow." Staying in "flow" became super important to me. I began to imagine myself riding a magic carpet, riding this incredible current carrying me through life. I let go of all expectations. I allowed myself to tap into something deep within, my higher self, and I allowed that to take over with grace and ease.

As I started meditating each morning, I began to feel calmer and more in control of my own life.

Up until this moment, for many months, I'd wake up with a rush of anxiety. My mind would swarm with everything I had to do: All the bills

I had to pay, preparing for court; showing up for my sister who was diagnosed with cancer at the same time I served my ex-husband the divorce papers; showing up for my three children who were just as shocked, confused, and heartbroken as I was to learn that divorce was inevitable. They were only ten, eleven and fifteen years old when the divorce started.

I used to fall asleep with that same rush of terror. However, after about only thirty days of meditating, I woke up with a feeling of inner peace. At first, I thought it was odd. I tried to bring on the feeling of anxiety, the feeling of being out of control. I couldn't bring it on. The meditation did during the divorce exactly what it did for me when I was diagnosed with cancer. I trusted in the present moment that everything was alright. I built upon that feeling of neutrality and acceptance to RISE into love, joy, and inner peace as my "constant," my new foundational feeling. My new and improved vibe.

Once I worked my way up to the frequency of love, joy, and inner-peace, I began to attract the most amazing people, places, and experiences. I'm surrounded by the most amazing people. I have grown my personal and professional coaching business over the last few years in extraordinary ways. My relationship with my children is magnificent. My alignment with who I truly am at the "soulular" level is phenomenal.

We don't have to wait for a trainwreck-type situation to begin to live our best lives. You can remove your self-limiting beliefs, self-doubt, and low self-esteem by reprograming your subconscious mind. It just takes repetition and time.

Have a crystal-clear vision of exactly what you want in life. The sky is just the beginning. Write it down. Meditate on it every morning and every night. Keep it in your mind's eye, in a bubble right in front of you, at all times. Let go of the victim mentality of "I can't" and embrace the empowered mentality of "I CAN!" This is how you override the negative beliefs you've been holding onto in your subconscious since childhood.

Through repeatedly reading your vision statement, meditating on it, and feeling as if what you want is happening right now, you can become unstoppable. You become comfortable in your own skin. You know yourself wholly, fully aligned with who you truly are. When you follow the Golden Rule, which I tweaked from "Treat others the way YOU want to be treated" to "Treat others the way THEY want to be treated," you become a force of nature with which to be reckoned. You will transform in ways you never could've imagined and it's absolutely beautiful.

A few months ago, my twenty-five-year-old son looked at me, and with all due respect, he said, "Mom, it's not normal for someone to be that happy." He was referring to me. I said, "Brendan, isn't it a shame that this world programs us to be miserable, to conform, to commiserate, to embrace the victim mindset, when all we must do is make a small shift subconsciously, and all that changes?"

Happiness becomes the norm. Optimism and hope are the new go-to regarding solutions. Enthusiasm makes life's journey so much more exciting. Exchange fear for gratitude. You'll never learn this in school. I'm here to show you the better way if that is what you want."

What is it that you want? What would you like to reprogram in your subconscious mind that is holding you back from living your best life? Would you like love, joy, and inner-peace to be your go-to feeling every day, enveloped in enthusiasm, optimism, and hope, as opposed to fear, lack, scarcity, worry, and hopelessness? It's all about mindset and how we program our subconscious.

If you'd like help with this, please reach out to me. I'm just a phone call away. My whole brand is "Life On Track Personally and Professionally." You aren't successful if you're making lots of money, but your personal life is suffering, and vice versa. Feel free to reach out to me to discuss the many ways I can help you. And always remember, to live onward and upward!

ERIN LEY

About Erin Ley: As Founder and CEO of Onward Productions, Inc., Erin Ley has spent the last thirty years as an Author, Professional Speaker, Personal and Professional Empowerment Coach, and Success Coach predominantly around mindset, vision, and decision. Founder of many influential summits, including "Life On Track," Erin is also the host of the upcoming online streaming T.V. show, *Life On Track with Erin Ley*, which is all about helping you get into the driver's seat of your own life.

They call Erin "The Miracle Maker!" As a cancer survivor at age twenty-five, single mom of three at age forty-seven, and successful entrepreneur at age fifty, Erin has shown thousands upon thousands across the globe how to become victorious by being focused, fearless, and excited about life and your future! Erin says, "Celebrate life and you'll have a life worth celebrating!"

To see more about Erin and the release of her fourth book, "WorkLuv: A Love Story," along with her "Life On Track" Course and Coaching Programs, please visit her website.

Author's Website: *www.ErinLey.com*

Book Series Website: *www.The13StepsToRiches.com*

Fatima Hurd

SUBCONSCIOUS DESIRE

The subconscious Mind is the direct link to God. Napoleon Hill explains how the finite mind of humans can draw power from the "Infinite Intelligence," also known as God, the Source, or the Universe.

When I think of my subconscious mind, I think of it as a messenger that delivers my letters, intentions, or prayers to God. As Napoleon Hill explains in *Think and Grow Rich*, "It alone is a medium through which prayer may be transmitted to a source capable of answering prayer. However, as powerful as the subconscious mind is, it lacks direction. When the impulses of thought are being fired through, distinguish the positive thoughts from negative thoughts. The subconscious mind simply accepts anything you send through. But the thoughts that take form are usually the ones that carry the weight of emotion with them.

Thought is the vessel in which our emotions are delivered to the Infinite Intelligence for processing. When we maintain a higher level of vibration as we draw the power of infinite intelligence, we transmute our desires into physical equivalents, as stated by Napoleon Hill in *Think and Grow Rich*.

This is why I love creating vision boards! As mentioned in my previous chapters, I began doing vision boards in 2007 when I lost my job. I remember reading Jack Canfield's book, *The Success Principles*. This was the first time I had ever heard of a vision board. I brought into fruition 90% of the things on that board. And after reading Napoleon

Hill's *Think and Grow Rich*, I understood the secret sauce of what I did to manifest my desire from that year.

Napoleon Hill describes how the subconscious mind is susceptible to influence by impulses of thought that are mixed with feeling or emotion rather than by those originating solely in the reasoning portion of the mind. He describes the seven major positive and negative emotions to which the subconscious mind reacts quickly.

I will explain how this helped manifest all my desires that I voluntarily submitted to my subconscious mind through my vision board. My son was born on Friday, December 14th. I was on maternity leave. As I mentioned, I ended the relationship with his dad and felt all alone until the day when my son was born. Looking at my son and his beautiful little eyes, and just being in awe and wonder about this little human, made everything, all my worries, my problems, my sadness seem petty and insignificant as my heart was full and overwhelmed with so much love for this little human.

As we got closer to Christmas, the thought came to mind: will this little guy ever know love from a father figure? At the time, things were still a little raw from my breakup with his dad. The breakup was bad, and that caused his dad to become completely distant from my son. My son will always know his mother's love, but he deserves more—he deserves a father's love!

Even though the thought started as a negative emotion of fear, the emotion of love transmuted that emotion. I declared that very moment that my son will know what is to be loved by a father figure, a blessing denied to me not once but twice. He was going to have a father who understood and loved him unconditionally and would show him a love that left him feeling worthy and deserving of being loved!

As I journaled, another burning desire surfaced: Love. Even though I thought I didn't want anything to do with being in love again, my human desire to connect with another was superseded. I wanted to love and be loved; that person would be someone who adored my son as much as they did me. When I thought about it, I was full of hope and possibility.

There was no lack of faith and the certainty that my son and I deserved someone like that.

The feelings and emotions were powerful. I would meditate on it and see him, never his face but his voice and mannerisms. I held that vision in my mind—how he was excited to be in my son's life; how he was loving, caring, and understanding. He loved being our protector and provider; in return, we loved and adored him. We were a perfectly imperfect family.

That image of the man I had seen in my mind was transferred to my vision board. I described him with great detail and with emotions as though I had already lived it. This image of him was embedded deep into my subconscious mind. It served as a magnet to attract now my husband into my life, and he is true as I had described him.

I still have that vision board. It was a very simple vision board but powerful indeed. My mind broke free of the limitation and drew the power of infinite intelligence to manifest my true heart's desire. What was revealed is that through my desire to manifest a wonderful life for my son, I, too, wanted to love again. These thoughts that carried these positive emotions influenced my subconscious and quickly manifested my husband in my life.

That is one of my strongest manifestations, and I attributed it to the strong desire I had that my son deserved an extraordinary father in his life. I also feel that this thought was influenced by the lack of a father who cared for and adored me. I knew exactly what I wanted for my son; I had that clarity and could tap into my subconscious mind to bring it to fruition. I tapped into six of the seven emotions Napoleon Hill talks about in *Think and Grow Rich* when I created my vision board, which transformed the negative emotion of fear into faith!

FATIMA HURD

About Fatima Hurd: Fatima is a personal brand photographer and was featured in the special edition of Beauty & Lifestyle's mommy magazine.

Fatima specializes in personal branding photographs dedicated to helping influencers and entrepreneurs expand their reach online with strategic, creative, inspiring, and visual content. Owner of a digital consulting agency, Social Branding Digital Solutions, Fatima helps professionals with all their digital needs.

Fatima holds ten years of photography experience. An expert in her field, she hosts workshops to teach anyone who wants to learn how to use and improve their skills with DSLR and on manual mode.

Hurd is also a mother of three, wife, certified Reiki master, and certified crystal healer. She loves being out in nature, enjoys taking road trips with her family, and loves meditation and yoga on the beach.

Author's Website: *www.FatimaHurd.com*

Book Series Website: *www.The13StepsToRiches.com*

Frankie Fegurgur

IF YOU BECAME A BILLIONAIRE, WHO WOULD YOU TELL?

You don't get what you want out of life; you get what you expect. No, I'm not talking about walking around with a sense of entitlement. No one is handing out free money just because people think they deserve it. Consider what you want from your life, versus the minimum that you are willing to accept.

People say they want money, fame, power, relationships, and even social impact, but when you evaluate their behavior and actions toward achieving those things, there is a disconnect. This is disheartening because when we are children, anything is possible, at least until our upbringing tells us otherwise. These limitations placed upon us by our peers, family, culture, and environment set the tone for how we interact with the world and what we believe we are worthy of.

To improve your financial outcomes, you'll first need to understand how your subconscious mind embedded your unique money limitations. One way to identify these patterns is by utilizing The Klontz Money Script Inventory. You can then determine where your beliefs about money came from and how best to change them.

I'm going to employ an amalgam of my real clients to share examples of the four money scripts: Avoidance, Worship, Status, and Vigilance. You may relate to some or all of these, particularly on an emotional level. The strong emotions associated with your memories are what drove your subconscious to create the blueprint that you operate from without conscious effort. Awareness is enough to interrupt the pattern and create space to install new patterns. Then, we can let go of beliefs that no longer serve us, even if they have been rooted for decades. Let's start with Amy's Avoidance.

Amy avoids dealing with money. She grew up in a small town, hearing that "money is the root of all evil." One of her earliest memories is the look of contempt on her mom's face, as she whispered about someone in town whose family "comes from money." Amy enjoys helping people and went to college to become a mental health professional, taking on lots of student loan debt. She tries to avoid thinking about money and sometimes forgets to pay her bills. This makes her afraid to check her bank account balance, and she is ashamed to ask for help from a financial professional.

After burning out from public service, Amy decided to open a private practice. Whenever it's time to bill her clients, she tenses up and has trouble justifying her fees. She'd rather not talk about price at all, and significantly undercharges for her level of expertise. She struggles to keep the lights on, having chronically under-earned her entire career. Even when she finally felt like she was getting ahead, some unforeseen expenses almost wiped her out. She would love to take on wealthier clients but has difficulty approaching and connecting with them. They always seem to ghost her. Secretly, she doesn't believe she deserves more money.

Will worships money. He equates possessing money with happiness and even love. His first job was working for tips, and he's been hooked on making fast money ever since. His wife laments that they never get to have any fun because he sacrifices family time to work overtime. When it comes to starting a business, Will subscribes to the mantra: "It takes money to make money" and blames the bad economy or the conglomerates playing unfairly as to why he isn't more successful.

He is waiting to "be discovered" and handed millions of dollars. Because of his distrust of traditional banking systems, he has neglected to build long-term investments. He will most likely end up depending on government assistance when he is older because he can't keep up with the rising costs of living.

Will's children grow up not understanding how credit works and fall prey to credit card debt as soon as they become adults. They will feel pressured to give their aging father money every month, because of all the sacrifices Will made raising them. When they don't give him money, he withholds his affection. For Will, cash will always be king.

Susie is all about status. She must have the newest phone, the shiniest car, and the gaudiest clothing. She grew up poor and was teased for her hand-me-downs and wished she could be like her favorite social media influencers. Susie never went to college but landed a high-paying sales job. She occasionally loses money by chasing the hottest cryptocurrency or getting scammed in a get-rich-quick scheme. It's not enough to own high-end luxuries, Susie needs to be seen living the good life because how she is perceived is tied to her self-worth. Conversations with her are always superficial. She watches A LOT of reality TV. She talks about celebrities as if she knows them. She always seems to know what they are doing, what they own, and who they are dating.

As far as who she is dating, Susie has two children from a previous relationship, but things didn't work out. She has conflated expectations of her future spouse's income and lifestyle. She could never settle for an "ordinary" partner. Susie's children are also materialistic. From the time they were born, they wore name-brand shoes and did photoshoots with Susie in matching outfits. They tease and look down on their classmates who have a more modest upbringing.

Victor is vigilant with all aspects of his finances. He is always looking for the best deal. He despises debt, especially credit cards. Victor waits until he's saved enough cash to buy something instead of financing it. He isn't flashy; in fact, his friends and family have no idea he has amassed a seven-figure net worth. He is the quintessential "millionaire next door." Victor's wife complains that he is too frugal and that he should loosen up, considering they have plenty of money saved for emergencies.

While Victor has saved plenty of money for retirement, he won't spend much of it for fear of running out. He will work part-time after retirement just in case the economy crashes. His only child went to a respectable college, working part-time to minimize the financial burden. They graduated with a "safe" degree in accounting and will most likely work for the same company for the next thirty years unless they embrace what they want, not what their father, Victor, wants for them.

Please reread the examples with your full attention. It's normal to recognize a part of yourself in each of them. While I mostly shared the limiting beliefs they exhibited, there are also positive aspects to their behavior. Amy develops an awareness of the power of money to help people. Will has a strong work ethic. Susie appreciates the finer things in life. Victor is humble about his net worth. If you want to do well for yourself, and positively impact the community at exceedingly greater levels, I encourage you to become aware of and embody the best parts of your money mindset.

Attention is the number one currency of this century. Ask any social media company why they pay millions of dollars to content creators. They'll admit that it's because they want your attention. Once they have it, they can influence your behavior for their gain.

You're done with outside forces controlling your actions. You're done with worrying about the future. You're done with mentally living in the past. Turn your attention to the present moment. As you consider the money scripts that previously held you back, command an alternate focus and outcome. It will take a combination of repetition and the right fuel in the form of emotions.

To upgrade your subconscious beliefs about money, generate a positive emotional drive strong enough to motivate you to act. Imagine what it is like to live abundantly instead of just surviving. In the past, you may have struggled, and now it's time to receive. While this change has the potential to be instant, don't be discouraged if it's not.

We all know someone who wakes up one morning and decides to change everything in their life all at once. They quit their job, move across the country, exercise until they pass out, and totally cut out sugar and gluten. You know who I'm talking about: they always take it to the extreme—only to quit or fall apart shortly thereafter. This all-or-nothing mentality comes from a place of lack. Stressed-out people behave irrationally. Instead, recommit to keeping small promises to yourself.

Give your subconscious evidence to believe you when you state your intentions of abundance. Upgrading your money mindset starts with putting your attention on the patterns you see in your current financial situation and creating space for change without judgment. If the money script examples from Amy, Will, Susie, and Victor weren't enough to start the process, then I'd invite you to answer the original question from my title and consider how you arrived at your response: "If you became a billionaire, who would you tell?"

FRANKIE FEGURGUR

About Frankie Fegurgur: Frankie's "burning desire" is helping people retire with dignity. Frankie distills the lessons he has learned over the last fifteen years and empowers our youth to make better financial decisions than the generation before them. This is a deeply personal mission for him—he was born to high-school-aged parents, and money was always a struggle. Frankie learned that hard work alone wasn't the key to financial freedom and sought a more fulfilling path. Now, he serves as the COO of a nonprofit financial association based in the San Francisco Bay Area, teaching money mindfulness. He, his wife, and their two children can be found exploring, volunteering, and building throughout their community.

Author's Website: *www.FrankMoneyTalk.com*

Book Series Website: *www.The13StepsToRiches.com*

Fred Moskowitz

UNDERSTANDING HOW BEST TO WORK WITH OUR SUBCONSCIOUS MIND

When you are awake or asleep, your subconscious mind is busy at work.

While you sleep, your conscious mind is at rest. On the other hand, your subconscious mind is still hard at work, twenty-four hours a day, seven days a week. It is handling your bodily functions, heartbeat, digestive system, breathing, as well as the growth and repair throughout your body. Also, it is working hard at solving problems. This is why sometimes you might wake up with an idea, a thought, vivid dreams, or an inspiration.

When this happens, it is a good habit to take action and quickly write down those ideas. Otherwise, there is an ultra-high risk of them becoming lost and forgotten forever. I like the idea of keeping a pen and notepad ready at the bedside table, so that I can write down some notes when I wake up with an idea in the middle of the night. If we don't do this, the thought can quickly be forgotten. It is amazing to sometimes wake up and see what I had written down the night before on that notepad; if I had not captured it, the thought could otherwise have been forgotten.

At its most basic level, the priority of the subconscious is to protect you from pain, and to move you towards pleasure. As part of this protection, it prioritizes certainty and familiarity over anything that is unknown, uncertain, or unfamiliar. This is the main reason why many people naturally resist change in their lives, because it feels very uncomfortable.

Our subconscious mind is a very powerful force, and if we understand how to best utilize it, then there is no limit to what we can create or achieve. Every single invention, revolutionary concept, or idea started out in the beginning as a thought, a vision, or a dream. Let's look at some examples: the automobile, the light bulb, the smartphone, the library system, the airplane, the Phillips head screw and screwdriver. Just about any example that you can think of, know that it started out as a thought in a person's mind.

The power of the subconscious mind is also discussed by Wallace D. Wattles in his book, *The Science of Getting Rich*. Wattles impresses on us the following idea:

"There is a Thinking Stuff from which all things are made, and which, in its original state, permeates, penetrates, and fills the inner spaces of the Universe. A thought in this Substance produces the thing that is imaged by the thought. Man can form things in his thought, and, by impressing his thought upon Formless Substance, can cause the thing he thinks about to be created."

The Influences on The Subconscious Mind

There are some major influencing factors which help to shape, form, and influence the subconscious mind. We will briefly touch on them here:

Words: The words that we speak, hear, and read. Words come from so many external sources, such as books, letters, music lyrics, video and film, the news and media, and most especially from the conversations with others around you. Take a moment to consider some of the words and the messaging that you are exposed to on a regular basis. Are they uplifting and positive, or are they degrading and negative? Have you ever noticed what happens when you turn on the news or social media platforms, and you quickly get sucked in and mesmerized? Think about and observe what types of messaging you are being exposed to on a daily basis.

Beliefs: Our beliefs are the ideas that we hold as truths. Unfortunately, many of us have developed limiting beliefs resulting from the

129

environment we grew up in, or because of things that certain authority figures (for example, family members, teachers, religious leaders, sports coaches) told us about ourselves. You are going to grow up just like your mother/father. You are good at math. You are not going to amount to anything in life. You are a gifted and creative person. You have a unique ability.

Beliefs are what we think is possible for ourselves, or what is possible for someone else. What ideas do we accept, reject, or create? What are the things that we dream about and visualize? How much do you feel your time is worth? Do you suffer from "imposter syndrome?" Has anyone ever suggested to you that you were "playing small?" Did you agree or disagree with them? Oftentimes, it takes the observant eye of a good coach or mentor to see something in us that we did not see for ourselves.

"Whether you think you can, or think you can't, you're right."
~ Henry Ford

Image: Image is the way in which you see yourself, your confidence, and your self-worth. If you think about your environment as a mirror, it will show you what thoughts you have of yourself. The self-talk that runs in our mind is a powerful indicator and reinforcement of our self-image. This is why it is often said that what we focus our attention on will expand. The powerful idea is that if we change the image we have about ourselves, we will change the results we are achieving in life. Think of your image as your internal thermostat, and that as a human, you have the ability to adjust the set-point (direction) of where you want to go in life. The results that you are achieving in life are just like a thermometer, showing you where you are, showing you the progress that you are making.

When Something is on the Tip of Your Tongue

We have all experienced or felt this sensation at some point. In the middle of a conversation, we suddenly struggle to remember a person's name, a word, or something else. Your mind begins to race with intensity. The questions appear in your head: What was that name? What was that word? Where did I put my keys? You are absolutely certain that you do know that word—it was right there. You absolutely know that person's name—you can even visualize an image of their face right in front of you. And the funny thing is that the harder we focus on trying to remember the thing we forgot, the more difficult it becomes to remember. We keep pushing; we try harder. With a little more force, we keep trying to remember, and it becomes more and more frustrating.

And then, if you take your attention off remembering the word, the name, or the thing, and go focus on something else for a while. This is where we allow our subconscious mind to take over and continue to work in the background. We are now focused on a different task or activity and we gradually become more relaxed. The frustration that we felt has now had a chance to dissipate. Time goes by, perhaps five minutes or five hours have passed. We are focused on other activities and the memory of having forgotten that thing is long gone. Our subconscious mind continues hard at work, searching in all of its internal memory banks. We don't think about it unless we focus our attention on it, just like breathing.

Then, all of a sudden, it comes right back to us, out of the blue! Our subconscious mind does not fail us, and it does deliver. The forgotten name, the word, the thing—it now comes right back to us when we least expect it.

The same concept can be applied to solving a problem, seeking a solution, or creating a new idea. It all starts with having a definite end in mind, even when we do not know all the details about how we are going to connect the dots, and then trusting in ourselves and in our abilities.

When we hand over something to our subconscious mind, it will continue to work on it, even while we are focused on other tasks, including while we sleep. Napoleon Hill, in his book *Think and Grow Rich*, describes about the subconscious mind that you "cannot entirely control your subconscious mind, but you can voluntarily hand over to it any plan, desire, or purpose which you wish transformed into concrete form."

Taking Action

When a thought or an idea suddenly comes to you from what seems to be "out of the blue" or unexpected, it is usually coming right from your subconscious mind. How often do you have thoughts like this that come into your mind? How often do you wake up in the middle of the night with thoughts like these: The thought of reaching out to a friend, family member, or colleague that you have not spoken with in some time; an idea for a new business, product, or service that you could bring to the marketplace; a new goal or objective that you would like to begin to pursue; a task that still needs completion, that had been forgotten.

I have found that the best way to benefit from this is to immediately take action on the thought, even if it is in a small way. Right away, take a small step towards that thought. Make the call. Send a quick message. Schedule a meeting. Order the book. Sign up and register for the workshop or course.

The longer that you wait to take action, the more likely it is that you will quickly forget, procrastinate, or fail to move forward with the implementation. The best chance for success is to stop what you are doing and to immediately take one small step to kick things off before you even get up out of your chair.

In summary, your subconscious mind is like a powerful computer that is always working on your behalf. Learn about the various inputs and outputs that you have to work with, and utilize them to your advantage. And most importantly, be ready to take action on those outputs!

FRED MOSKOWITZ

About Fred Moskowitz: Fred Moskowitz is a bestselling author, investment fund manager, and speaker who is on a personal mission to teach people about the power of investing in alternative asset classes, such as real estate and mortgage notes, showing them the way to diversify their capital into investments that are uncorrelated from Wall Street and the stock markets.

Through his body of work, he is teaching investors the strategies to build passive income and cash flow streams designed to flow into their bank accounts. He's a frequent event speaker and contributor to investment podcasts.

Fred is the author of *The Little Green Book of Note Investing: A Practical Guide for Getting Started with Investing in Mortgage Notes* and contributing author in *1Habit To Thrive in a Post-Covid World*.

Author's Website: *www.FredMoskowitz.com*

Book Series Website: *www.The13StepsToRiches.com*

Gina Bacalski

THE PATH THROUGH THE TREES

I was at the end of my wit's end with Ashton. As the lead teacher for the three-to-four-year-old classroom, I was out of ideas of trying to get one of my young pupils to stop hitting his classmates. Whenever he got the tiniest bit upset, he would hit, punch, or push one of his friends. His latest victim would cry and run to me, and Ashton, yelling and crying himself, would be sent to Time Out, where I told him to think about what he did and why he was in time-out, yet again.

Ashton spent A LOT of time in Time Out.

I grew more and more weary.

As a part of my Continuing Education courses that all Early Childhood educators, registered and licensed in the state of Utah, are required to complete, I eagerly took a Discipline Course, anxious to find something new that I could use to help my Ashton finally stop hitting his classmates.

I was not prepared for what my instructor, Ms. Shanna, had planned.

She boldly declared she never used time out in any of her classrooms, and she encouraged us to do the same.

What in the world? Was she joking? Not use Time Out? How did she retain order? How did she punish the bad kids that needed to be taught a lesson?

Ms. Shanna then explained a fundamental principle that changed my life.

Our brains are hardwired to *receive* instruction, not to *exclude* instruction. With kids, that means if I see a child standing on the table, which is against the rules of the classroom, instead of saying, "Don't stand on the table," she encouraged us to instead say, "Put your feet on the floor."

In other words, it was much more impactful to tell my young pupils what I *want* them to do, instead of telling them what I *don't* want them to do.

She then encouraged us to eliminate the words "Don't," "Stop," and "No" from our vocabulary when we were instructing or correcting behavior in our classes.

She asked a very poignant question that I still remember to this day.

"If the only thing your kids hear from you, is "don't," "stop," and "no," all negative words, how do you think that will impact their day?"

That made me pause and think. I loved my kids. I didn't want them to hear only negativity from me. But upon reflection, with some of my kids, besides "Circle time" and "Reading Time," that's the main thing they heard.

I quickly started a list of phrases I regularly told my kids as we went about our day, and ways to modify it to make it a positive instruction instead:

- Don't run – Walking feet, please.
- Stop talking – Wait your turn to talk.
- Don't color on the table – Keep all markers and crayons on your paper.
- Don't run in the street – Feet and bodies on the sidewalk.

I loved this idea. I could do this.

She then shifted back to her "Don't use Time Out" ideology. I thought *that* idea was a load of bunk.

I shut it down in my head before I even heard her explanation. I remember writing down her instructions and thinking there was no way it was going to work. I even shook my head in disdain several times. By the time she was done explaining the whole thing, I looked at my page of notes and got frustrated.

Fine! I thought harshly. *I'll try your stupid plan and I'll prove you wrong.*

The next day, I put her plans in place.

The "don't," "stop," and "no" things were more difficult than I thought. I really had to think about things before I said them. The more I did it, though, the easier it got. My kids responded much better to these instructions than the "Don't Instructions" I was using before.

The No Time Out thing? The jury was still out.

At free-play time, sure enough, within a few moments, Ashton got mad and hurt a friend. Following the instructions, and a hefty eye roll, I went over to the scene of the "crime" and sat down. I put Ashton on one knee and the kid he hit, Morgan, on my other knee, and held them both until they were calmed down.

"Buddy, I see you're upset, and you hit Morgan—what happened?" I asked.

"Morgan wouldn't let me play with the blue car even though I got it first!"

"I hear you. If someone took something that I was playing with, I would be upset, too. It's okay to be upset. It's not okay to hurt Morgan. What is something you should have done instead?"

He didn't know. He honestly didn't know. After all those times he had to sit in Time Out, and I told him to think about what he did, he still didn't know what to do when he was upset or mad. Wow. Teaching fail on my part.

"Did you ask Morgan to give it back?" I asked.

"Yes, and she said no, and she moved it away so I couldn't grab it."

"I see. It's still not okay to hit your friend. Next time something like this happens, let's make a plan. Instead of hitting Morgan, stomp your foot on the ground and run straight to me, and I'll help you solve it. Is that a good plan? Can we do that?"

"Yes," Ashton agreed.

"I know you can do this and make good choices. You're an awesome kid!" I gave him a high-five.

"Now. Is it okay that you hit Morgan?"

"No."

"You're right, it's not okay to hit. I won't let you hit Morgan, and I won't let Morgan hit you. But because you hit Morgan, we're going to take a break from the car area for a little while. You may read a book or work with puzzles for now, and we'll try the car area again in a few minutes. Which activity would you like to do?"

Ashton didn't love the idea of not being able to play with the cars anymore, but I explained that next time if he does our plan, he wouldn't have to leave. He marched over to the book area and sat down.

This went on for about three weeks. We went over the plan again and again. More high fives, more spending time in the book area after a fight, but overall, a happier Ashton.

One day, we were in the gym, and the kids were playing with hoops and balls. Ashton had a blue hoop, his favorite color. Morgan, ran up to Ashton, pulled the blue hoop out of his hands, and ran away. Ashton yelled at Morgan to come back, but she did not.

I held my breath and slowly started making my way over to where they were.

He started for Morgan, then stopped, stomped his foot, turned around and ran straight to me! He yelled that Morgan had taken his hoop.

"Buddy, you did it!" I yelled as I scooped him up and twirled him around. We clapped, and I told him how proud I was of him. Ashton laughed and jumped when he high-fived me.

I then called Morgan over to us and made her give Ashton back his hoop and Ashton happily resumed playing. I had Morgan follow me over to the rug area to read books until she could try playing nice with friends again in a few moments.

I was proven wrong. Miss Shanna's plan worked. I wrote a note to Miss Shanna thanking her and telling her that I, too, had stopped using time out, *permanently*.

Shortly thereafter, I got promoted to Assistant Director and put in charge of all the preschool classrooms. I quickly put Miss Shanna's No-Time-Out protocol in place in every classroom at the center. The energy and vibrations shift of the entire school was palpable.

Now back to Miss Shanna's question: "If the only thing your kids hear from you, is 'don't,' 'stop,' and 'no," all negative words, how do you think that will impact their day?"

I'm going to modify it slightly. Please read it again, carefully. "If the only thing YOU hear from you is 'don't,' 'stop,' and 'no,' all negative words, how do you think that will impact YOUR day?"

From teaching this principal to children, I've also learned how to shift my internal self-talk.

Instead of saying to myself, "Don't eat those cookies, stop eating sugar, no soda," I say, "Eat a fruit or vegetable if you're still hungry, make healthy food choices, drink your favorite healthy beverage."

This is something professional skiers have learned as well. When skiing through a wooded area, if they think "Don't hit a tree," they will always hit a tree. Remember, that's the way our brains are hardwired to work. So, instead of focusing on the trees, they focus on the path. They think "Follow the path around the trees," and they safely make it down the mountain.

As Napoleon Hill said, "Positive and Negative emotions cannot occupy the mind at the same time."

How will focusing on the *path*, not the *trees* in everything you do in life, work for you?

GINA BACALSKI

About Gina Bacalski: Gina is a Real Estate Agent, licensed since June 2018. Her background is in Early Childhood Education where she received her Child Development Associate from the state of Utah and has an AS from BYU-Idaho. For the past seventeen years, Gina thoroughly enjoyed her experience in the service industry helping families in the gifted community.

In 2019, Gina helped Jon Kovach Jr. in his launch of Champion Circle. She brings her genuine love for people, high attention to detail, and strives to exceed client's expectations to the Real Estate industry.

Gina married the man of her dreams, Jay Bacalski, in San Diego, in 2013. The Bacalski's love entertaining friends and family, going on hikes, and attending movies and plays. When Gina isn't helping her clients navigate the real estate world, she will most often be found dancing and listening to BTS, watching KDramas and writing fantasy, sci-fi and romance novels.

Author's Website: *www.MyChampionCircle.com/Gina-Bacalski*

Book Series Website: *www.The13StepstoRiches.com*

Griselda Beck

SWITCHING OFF AUTO PILOT

The Subconscious Mind: the parts of your mind you are not yet aware of, which contain the programming for your autopilot state of mind. You are either intentionally creating your life or you are simply reacting to the life your autopilot mode created. ***Question is…***

Do you want to create your life or react to it?

I'm willing to bet that since you are reading this right now, the answer is the former. You are powerful and you're reading this to sharpen those exact skills. The first step toward making any change is awareness. At some point there is an *awakening*, a realization that you're not where you want to be. Just like when you are driving and "zone out," aka go on autopilot and all of sudden "awaken" to realize that you have changed lanes, or you are much further than you remember, or simply realize you were somehow "asleep" and missed something in that time lapse.

In one unexpected second, you are on autopilot and in one equally unexpected second you are back—just like that. Pause here…take that in. Reflect on some of those moments now.

When we are doing activities that we've done hundreds of times, we can do things without thinking. The way we move about life is no different. Our belief system is a set of beliefs we hold as true because this is what we've always known them to be. We live our life according to these beliefs and we will go on to produce a life according to those beliefs if they remain unchallenged.

When we open our minds to new people, cultures, ways of thinking through travel, conversation, education, reading, connecting with new people, etc., we begin to challenge those beliefs. At the very least, we become "aware" that somewhere, someone, may think differently and that another perspective exists.

Have you ever had the experience of a "favorite" something until you try a new something and that now becomes your new favorite? Same concept. Upon trying the new favorite, you became aware of another amazing option, and, now, based on re-evaluation, you prefer that new option.

So, how can you know what is the best for you if you do not expand your thinking and exposure to new possibilities? How can you know what you truly want if you are not even aware of what you are choosing each day? When was the last time you paused and really took inventory of how you feel?

Here are some possible signs you've been living life on automatic, aka **reacting to life**:

- You work in the job you "should" have.
- You dread going to work more often than not.
- You feel trapped in a relationship.
- OR you're single and *avoiding* feeling trapped in a relationship.
- Your relationships always end the same way or for the same reason.
- You're fatigued and tired all the time. You have unexplained low energy.
- You're feeling lost, lonely and unmotivated.
- You're always having to "fight" for what you want.
- OR you're "working hard" to *make things work.*
- You're not feeling well, but no matter how many tests your doctor runs, no one can figure out a proper diagnosis.

- You're stuck in a routine, just going through the motions…day after day, rinse and repeat.
- You daydream and fantasize about what you really wish you could do or where you really want to go.
- You feeling depressed, anxious or both.
- You feel overwhelmed, or you are constantly second-guessing yourself.

Sound familiar? You are not alone. I've been there myself! I truly believe "autopilot mode" is the leading cause of disease, stress, divorce, and death. It's where dreams go to die.

On flip side, **creating life** looks like:

- Pinching yourself, because you cannot believe you have a "GET to do this AND get PAID for it" type of job.
- Living a lifestyle that has you excited to wake up in the morning.
- Being in a relationship that lights you TF up!
- An amazing sex life.
- Feeling free, happy and loved.
- Feeling like yourself—that confident and invincible feeling.
- You're easy going and not much can get you too ruffled up.
- People gravitate towards you because they feel energized and motivated around you.
- You're surrounded by amazing people doing amazing things.
- You are at peace.

Ok, so we all get it, and now the question is *how do we turn autopilot off?*

Step 1: Awareness: As you are reading this book, you are already aware.

Step 2: Take Inventory: What is your life like now? Rate each of the following on a scale from 1-10 (1 being "Sucks" and 10 being "Amazing"). For any that are less than 10, write just a few words (no more than one sentence) on what would make it a "10."

- Job/Career/Business:

- Finances:

- Sex Life:

- Relationships:

  - Romantic Partnership:

  - Friends/Social:

  - Family:

  - Self:

- Spiritual/Soul:

- Fun/Adventure:

Step 3: Vision: What do you want? Set the timer for ten minutes and write whatever comes to mind—just don't stop writing. Don't filter, judge, or edit your thoughts; simply put thoughts to paper as they are. I strongly encourage you to not limit yourself to only material things, but also to describe the "vibe" of what you want. Example: Rather than simply writing "I want a partner/husband/girlfriend, etc.," write that and add how you want to feel in that relationship. What do you want to experience? What would a date look like? What little things does this person do that make you feel so loved?

Step 4: Gap Analysis: What's missing in the vibe between where you are now in your experience of your life and where you want to be?

Step 5: Subconscious Mind: What is getting in the way? What is keeping you there? This is where our thought and behavior patterns and our beliefs systems get to move from unconscious to conscious awareness. Spend some time here thinking about it. This is not something that will necessarily come to mind immediately.

Some practices that may support this process are meditation, journaling, talk therapy, working with a coach, and group experience (such as masterminds, circles, and retreats). The simplest of these practices that has served me well? Asking out loud and giving my mind, body, and soul permission to share with me the answers to these questions. I used to think it was weird when people said God spoke to them or "the Spirit said…" or they'd "tune in" and pause for a minute as if the silent air was speaking to them….

AND YET, if we sit still long enough if we are open, the answers do, in fact, come—sometimes audible as a faint whisper, an inspired thought, or an unexpected "random" thought (I usually experience this). People refer to these answers as downloads, codes, the Holy Spirit's message, etc. I call it my intuition. Call it whatever works for you. These prompts are real, and they are the highest level of wisdom and guidance if we allow them to be.

Step 6: Take Action: Uncovering our limiting beliefs that lie deep in our subconscious mind is how we get off autopilot. Once you are aware, then you *have a choice, and choice is power*. This is where you make an action plan. Get support from a peer, mentor, and coach. Change is not easy and it takes practice and commitment. It takes changing thought patterns, habits, and your environment (i.e., people with whom you associate, job, media—what you watch, scroll, listen to, and read, etc.).

If you are living in a pattern of recreating the same feelings/experiences, well, now you are aware of it. This is where you have the power to turn off that autopilot switch…if you choose to. Most people in these situations, even with awareness and choice, will not choose to turn off that switch. Most will continue to go to a job they hate, spend time with people they don't like, and drain their energy. Most will stay single or in a relationship they resent.

Most people will choose to settle. Will you?

GRISELDA BECK

About Griselda Beck: Griselda Beck, M.B.A. is a powerhouse motivational speaker and coach who combines her executive expertise with transformational leadership, mindset, life coaching, and heart-centered divine feminine energy principles. Griselda empowers women across the globe to step into their power, authenticity, hearts, and sensuality, to create incredible success in their business and freedom in their lives. She creates confident CEOs.

Griselda's clients have experienced success in quitting their 9-5 jobs, tripling their rates, getting their first client, launching their first product, and growing their business in a way that allows them to live the lifestyle and freedom they want. She has been featured as a top expert on FOX, ABC, NBC, CBS, MarketWatch, and Telemundo and named on the Top 10 Business Coaches list by Disrupt Magazine.

Griselda is an executive with over fifteen years of corporate experience, founder of Latina Boss Coach and Beck Consulting Group, and serves as president for the nonprofit organization MANA de North County San Diego. She also volunteers her time teaching empowerment mindset at her local homeless shelter, Operation Hope-North County.

Author's Website: *www.LatinaBossCoach.com*

Book Series Website: *www.The13StepsToRiches.com*

Jason Curtis

THE FORCES OF INFINITE INTELLIGENCE

"THE SUBCONSCIOUS MIND WORKS DAY AND NIGHT. Through a method or procedure that is not yet understood, the subconscious mind draws upon the forces of Infinite Intelligence for the power with which it voluntarily transmutes one's desires into their physical equivalent, making use always of the most practical media by which this end may be accomplished."
~ Napoleon Hill

JASON CURTIS

About Jason Curtis: Jason has been a serial entrepreneur for fifteen years and has enjoyed serving and helping his fellow entrepreneurs build their businesses and win in this game of life —on purpose! Jason created On Purpose Coaching because he knew, through his life experiences, that he could create an impact in others. He focuses on helping his clients create better relationships with their customers. This fosters trust and rapport while generating customer loyalty.

Jason is a Navy veteran of six years. He has sailed the seas and oceans in serving his God and country. Curtis and his wife, Brianna, have been married for eight years, and they have two children.

Author's Website: *www.JasonLaneCurtis.com*

Book Series Website: *www.The13StepsToRiches.com*

Jeffrey Levine

THE POWER OF THE SUBCONSCIOUS MIND

Many of us have been brought up in a negative environment. By listening to the news and reading the newspaper, you are programmed at an early age to be negative. Things happen in school, such as kids pick on us and teachers criticize our performances. At home, parents say no and get upset with us. Given that we often don't have positive alternatives to those experiences, we are continually programmed with negativity year after year with no solution. Many times, we don't even realize this is happening to us.

That negative programming is what happened to me until the day I attended a national financial planning conference in Boston, Massachusetts. That was five years after I started my financial planning practice in Albany, New York. Since that was my first financial planning conference, I didn't know what to expect. I loved the conference, and the last speaker was Brian Tracy. Because I was attending a financial planning conference, I thought Brian was just another financial planning speaker. But he wasn't—he was more of a positivity coach.

Given my background, I was shocked at the topic of Brian's presentation: Positivity. Since it was like he was speaking in a foreign language, I wrote down every word. He kept mentioning that we all need to reprogram our brains daily because all our lives, we have been programmed negatively.

Since he kept mentioning reading a book and listening to audios over and over, that became my new programming. He pointed out that repetition would reprogram your subconscious mind, and results would start happening in your life. At the end of his session, he offered his latest book and three audios for $100. He had opened my mind to positivity programming and the potential of living a different life, so I quickly bought them.

On the way home from the conference, I started listening to the audios for the next two and a half hours. Then, I listened to them on the way to work, at my office, and on the way home. I literally listened to those cassettes two to three hours a day and read his book over and over. Even though nothing magical happened right away, I followed his instructions.

After about six months, everything with my personal and business life started changing. First, I started being more positive. I suddenly started attracting much better clients. Because of that, I ordered more of Brian Tracy's audio programs and books. I couldn't stop reading the books over and over and listening to his new CDs again and again for three to four hours each day. Brian Tracy's concept of repetition was definitely reprogramming my subconscious mind. The results were amazing. My practice grew more than 50% in the next few years, and I was like a new person.

I also started going to his live events, as well as those with Tony Robbins and Zig Ziglar. They all said the same thing: "Repetition is the mother of all skills." In a short time, I was a self-improvement speaker myself, as well as a financial consultant. I was invited to speak all over the world, including Puerto Rico, Barbados, and Hawaii. Before I knew it, I was co-authoring books and appearing on TV and radio shows all the time. Suddenly, I had an amazing practice and a wonderful personal life.

One day, I realized I could do the same thing with my financial field as I did with Brian Tracy's materials. I started reading financial books over and over and listening to financial experts on CD. I knew I was getting much better in every area of my practice. It seemed as though I was attracting more complicated financial cases, and because of my new knowledge, I was able to solve them easily. I also realized that cases that had once seemed impossible were now possible. Also, because of my self-improvement reading and tapes, I found that I was getting along better with people. It also seemed that clients were staying with my practice much longer than they had previously.

I realized that I could use Brian Tracy's repetition ideas with sports. Since golf is such a mental game, I thought if I bought books and CDs on the mental game of golf, I would improve. I kept reading books and listening to CDs on the subject. I would re-read books and listen to the CDs for months with great things happening. For example, while playing in the championship at my club, I was behind the leader almost the whole tournament. On the last hole, I was still behind by two strokes. Even though I didn't hit a good drive, my second shot was magical. Because I was 200 yards away from the green and facing many obstacles, I decided to hit my club that only goes 150 yards, just short of the green.

When I struck the ball, it took off like a rocket and landed on the green next to the cup for an easy three on the par four hole. It was my first birdie ever on the hole. The leader, because he saw what I did, shockingly missed the next two shots and made a six, enabling me to win by one stroke. I was the new club champion, which is something I never could have imagined. The crazy part of that was that I had never seen the previous champion miss any shots before. He was that good.

As I kept reading those books repeatedly and listening to CDs on golf mindset, similar results happened. Just for fun, my partner Chester and I entered the biggest tournament of the year in upstate New York. The previous year, we had finished last of more than 100 players. That morning, I woke up feeling relaxed and kept seeing pictures of myself hitting the ball perfectly. Since that had never happened before, I didn't know what to make of it.

For the first fifteen holes, I played perfect golf. I felt fantastic and every shot went exactly where I wanted it to go. Chester kept asking what I had eaten for breakfast. I knew it wasn't that, but that my reading and listening over and over was reprogramming my mind. After we finished, we went to the cocktail hour until our names were called for a playoff.

We went first on the playoff hole. After Chester hit the ball out of bounds, I hit an average drive while the other team had great drives. The other team and I reached the green in three. After they missed their putts and since my putt was very long, I decided not to make the putt but play smart for a tie and go to an extra hole. Even though I didn't try to make the putt, the ball turned unexpectedly to the left and went in—and we won the tournament. We all knew that the putt never went to the left and it always went to the right. However, sometimes things defy explanation.

For example, the bumblebee is not supposed to be able to fly, but it does.

If you want better results, you must reprogram your mind with books and CDs. You need to read the books over and over and listen to the CDs again and again. Since we need to reprogram our minds for different results, realize that you now know the secret. You can also have similar results in your life.

JEFFREY LEVINE

About Jeffrey Levine: Jeffrey is a highly skilled tax planner and business strategist, as well as a published author and sought-after speaker. He's been featured in national magazines and on the cover of Influential People Magazine and is a frequent featured expert on radio, talk shows, and documentaries. Jeffrey attended the prestigious Albany Academy for high school and then went on to the University of Hartford in Connecticut, the University of Mississippi Law School, and Boston University School of Law, and earned an L.L.M. in taxation. His accolades include features in *Kiplinger* and *Family Circle Magazine*, as well as a dedicated commentator for Channel 6 and 13 news shows, a contributor for the *Albany Business Review*, and an announcer for WGY Radio.

Jeffrey has accumulated more than thirty years of experience as a tax attorney and certified financial planner and has given in excess of 500 speeches nationally. Levine is the executive producer and cast member in the documentary *Beyond the Secret: The Awakening*.

Levine's most current work, *Consistent Profitable Growth Map*, is a step-by-step workbook outlining easy-to-follow steps to convert consistent revenue growth to any business platform.

Author's Website: *www.Strategies.org*

Book Series Website: *www.The13StepsToRiches.com*

Lacy & Adam Platt

THE ROLE OF THE SUBCONSCIOUS MIND & THE POSITIVE SUBCONSCIOUS MIND

THE ROLE OF THE SUBCONSCIOUS MIND

When we talk about the subconscious mind, a lot of people think that its only purpose is to keep our heart beating and to keep us from forgetting to breathe. What they don't consider, however, is the incredible power of our subconscious mind.

Here's something to consider: Did you know that every single thought, emotion or feeling that you have has already gone through your subconscious mind before it hits your conscious mind and you actually pay attention to it?!

So, that means every single plan you've ever had or desire you have felt first passed through a filter in your subconscious mind, was accepted, and then allowed to continue on its path to your conscious mind. Every stroke of genius or epiphany you have had came from somewhere! How do we explain that?

Many people have studied the subconscious mind and one thing that they keep finding is that, somehow, our subconscious mind is connected to a higher power, a higher version of ourselves, and that higher version is constantly and continuously plotting out and creating our future! It has been referred to as our higher intelligence, or even called infinite intelligence. As a religious person, I tend to go with infinite intelligence. This is because I know that when I have faith in my ability to figure things out, I force my brain to think higher. When I can go into this state of accessing that infinite intelligence, the inspiration and messages I receive are far beyond anything my conscious mind could ever even conceive.

I learned early on that my brain thinks differently than most. There was a time in my life when I felt like I was an outsider, like I didn't belong, but what I realize now is I just didn't understand what I was doing and, frankly, no one else around me did, either. There are a lot of times when I will have a stroke of inspiration on how to do something and when I suggest my approach to other people, they tell me it's impossible. I have learned that that usually just means it hasn't been done before. I used to let that stop me almost every time. It would cause me to question myself and why I thought to do it in the first place. Then, I realized my brain not only likes to create things to do, it likes to help people discover how to create a new way to do things.

I am notorious for finding a totally different path to take to get something done than most people would take. Again, I thought this made me weird or a freak. Now, I have learned that when people question my idea, it just means they are not the person that is going to help me create it. And that's okay! Not all people will understand you. Period. This will really just help you find the people that you need to surround yourself with—other people who think and create like you do!

When you can fine tune your ability to tap into that higher or infinite intelligence things, will start to change at a miraculous pace!

There is a saying, "We can't solve problems at the same level of thinking that we were at when we created the problems." Why? Because we have to think higher to come up with a solution to a problem that we created. We created the problem in the first place, then we hit a wall. Our conscious mind cannot create a solution to it—we have to dig deeper.

Oftentimes, we will have a problem that we will tell ourselves there is no solution for only to find a solution sometimes days or even weeks later. Why? It is because we get tired of sitting in that problem and we think on a higher level than we were when we created the problem to dig ourselves out of it. Silly, right?! I'm here to suggest that we tap into that higher intelligence the moment a problem presents itself, so that we can find a quicker and easier solution to our problems by engaging infinite intelligence! I promise with practice this gets easier!

~ Lacey Platt

THE POSITIVE SUBCONSCIOUS MIND

The mind is such a powerful tool. It can be used for either good or bad in your life, especially the subconscious part of your mind. Your mind is constantly taking in data and using it to make decisions about what to do. Many of these data points you don't even realize influence you because they only happen in the subconscious. The way we use this data influences how we respond and, ultimately, what we take action on.

You may have heard that what you focus on grows and what you neglect dies. This is true with how we use our subconscious. If we infuse into it negative thoughts and are always negative in what we think is going to happen to us, then guess what? The outcomes will be negative. However, if we can get into the habit of infusing positive thoughts into our subconscious, then we will have positive outcomes in our lives.

This is the formula on how it all works: Our thoughts create emotion, which in turn make us take action, and that creates results. In other words, thoughts = emotion = action = results.

If everything that comes into our subconscious mind is interpreted with negative thoughts, it will create negative emotions, and we will then either not do anything productive to create the life we want or we will do things that are counterproductive to our progression and our results will be negative.

On the other hand, if we can infuse positive energy into our subconscious, it will create positive emotions, helping us to take action towards goals or dreams and find ways to achieve what we want. The results are going to be amazing.

So, the question is: How do we infuse positivity into our subconscious? It takes effort and takes time to build that habit. With a subconscious infused with positive thoughts, your mind can find ways to take massive action toward the life you want to build for yourself. Here are my top three tools to infuse your subconscious with positive thoughts so it can create positive emotions:

- **Notice the Negative Thoughts & Change Them to Positive:** I was told by a coach of mine way back to keep a little notebook and every time a negative thought popped up in my head to write it down in the notebook. What this did was create awareness of all the negative things I was telling myself. Once you have that awareness, you can change them to positive thoughts. I did this by taking each negative thought and changing it to two positive thoughts.

  For instance, if you look in the mirror and say you look ugly, you change that into two positives. So, you flip that negative to two positive things: I am beautiful, and I have a great smile. By becoming aware of what negative things you are telling yourself and then flipping them to positive things, you create positivity in your subconscious mind.

- **Ask Yourself Better Questions:** Don't ask yourself negative questions. The mind is powerful and whatever you ask it, it will find an answer. If you ask yourself why your life is so messed up, guess what your mind will do? It will find reasons why your life is so messed up. But if you ask yourself what you have to be grateful for, your mind will find things to be grateful for. Or instead of asking why your spouse is so annoying, ask yourself why you are so lucky to have such an amazing spouse. The mind will find the answers to the questions we ask it. So, ask better positive questions.

- **Visualize Yourself in the Life You Want:** Don't visualize how you are going to get there—see yourself there and what that looks like, never doubting that you will get there. Don't ask yourself how or say, "When I have that life...." See yourself already there and have faith it will happen with no negative thoughts about it and infuse it with positive emotions.

Seeing yourself where you want to be and already envisioning yourself having that life creates amazing positive emotions and allows the subconscious mind to then find ways to take action to achieve those results. You are creating that positive reality in your mind before you create it in the physical world and that is really tapping into the power of your subconscious mind to have the results you want.

These habits won't happen overnight, but start implementing them and you will see amazing things happen in your life.

~ Adam Platt

LACEY & ADAM PLATT

About Lacey Platt: Lacey is an energetic, fun loving, super mom of five! She is an Achievement Coach, Speaker and new Bestselling Author who enjoys helping everyone she can by getting to know what their needs are and then loving on them in every way that she can. Her ripple effect and impact has touched the lives of so many and continues to reach more lives every single day. Allow Lacey to help you achieve your goals with proven techniques she has created and perfected over years of coaching. Her and her husband have built an amazing coaching business called Arise to Connect serving people all around the world.

About Adam Platt: Adam is an Achievement Coach, Speaker, Trainer, Podcast Host and now a Bestselling Author. Adam loves to help people overcome the things stopping them from having the life they really want. Adam owns and operates Arise to Connect. Adam believes that connection with yourself, others, and your higher power are the keys to achievement and greater success in life. He is impacting thousands of people's lives with his message and coaching. He lives in Utah with his five daughters and dog, Max.

Author's Website: *www.AriseToConnect.com*

Book Series Website: *www.The13StepsToRiches.com*

Louisa Jovanovich

MY THOUGHTS SERVE ME

I am in awe of our brilliant minds. I know I observe my thoughts. I also know there is a commentary in my brain that is literally telling me what I am seeing, hearing, and what my thoughts mean. I used to think they were all coming from one place. I have discovered that it is coming from many locations. For example, I listen to that still, small voice, and I ask myself—is this my voice of wisdom speaking or is it my voice of judgment? Sometimes it's my ego, other times it's my intuition. Is this something that is empowering me or disempowering me? I have learned to ask a lot of questions to break it down.

I know, too, that we get in our own way. I remember the day I was in a transformational course, and the leader was giving the instructions to the game we were about to play together. The minute I heard that math was required, I instantly shut down and had a hard time participating. This was supposed to be a transformational course. They were *not* going to tell me I was a dummy and I was *not* going to fail because of my math skills. I decided the best way to handle the situation was to blend in. No one would notice I was lost. As I have shared in previous chapters, how you do something is how you do everything. Being a wallflower was not working for me. I knew I was there for way more than being a girl who was blending in.

I have become very aware of how powerful my subconscious mind is and the role it plays in every experience. I have paid close attention to the sentences that come up and I unravel them instead of just taking them as a fact. For example, The idea that the only way to be very successful is to have graduated from college with straight A's or have to have parents

159

who know how to guide you to position yourself in the world with a great job and a great husband. You have to always look perfect, hair and nails intact. Your house has to be perfect—you must never leave a dirty dish in the sink and never leave your room without making your bed. This list could actually go on forever because there is no end to all the things I think I would need to live up to in order to be successful.

I have done hypnosis, guided visualizations, and daydreaming. Each of these practices help to access the power of the subconscious mind and get a better understanding of the inner self. Another excellent way to access the subconscious mind is to use affirmations. These are statements I repeat to myself daily to condition my mind into believing things about myself.

No matter which method you choose, the goal is to have a deeper connection to the subconscious mind and its infinite potential. Accessing the power of the subconscious mind can have many positive effects on the life you want to lead. Making decisions faster and with better outcomes are just some of the positive results. By becoming aware of my deepest thoughts and desires, I have been making decisions that are based on what truly matters to me.

I have found that by accessing the power of the subconscious mind, I have uncovered and resolved any blocks or negative patterns that have been preventing me from achieving my goals. Once I looked at all my beliefs, I created new beliefs. I have supporting evidence that helps me know I do not have to be perfect in any way to be successful. I can actually be myself exactly as I am and still accomplish incredible things.

Last night, I came across feedback from someone who has taken my course. It read, "Louisa is very caring and helpful. She truly loves what she does and her energy is contagious. She is a joy to know and take this journey with." This really spoke to me, because it is a very loving and kind thing to hear about myself.

Interestingly, I have been hearing similar sentiments at least once a week, but last night, the woman's comment moved me to collect the similar compliments I have received so far. They are all evidence that I am showing up in the world exactly as I am, flaws and all, and making a positive difference in the lives of others.

In his book, *Think and Grow Rich*, Napoleon Hill describes the subconscious mind as a creative "servant" that works constantly, night and day, to carry out the instructions it receives from the conscious mind. He states that it can store memories and habits, recall past experiences, and make all sorts of mental associations and connections based on our input.

Hill believed that the subconscious can be trained to bring forth our most desired goals and help us achieve success if we give it the proper instruction through autosuggestion, prayer, and meditation. He emphasizes that this inner power is one of our greatest allies in achieving success, and if we harness it correctly, it can lead us to the path of riches we desire. His book provides the training we need in order to put these techniques into practice.

I was at an event a few months ago where I was going to be interviewed on stage. Microphones, cameras, and recording devices were everywhere. Based on my old beliefs, I was nervous and actually afraid. I thought about what I was going to say and how I was going to say it. Was I going to mess up because I would be terrified being up there? These were my thoughts until I stepped onto the stage. At that point, there was so much going on preparing for me to speak that I got wrapped up in all that, and the fearful thoughts and insecurity just dropped away.

Once the mic had been placed onto my blouse, the interview process began. As the interviewer asked me questions, I answered them very naturally. It went very quickly and was over before I realized it. I took some photos as I was leaving the stage, and afterwards I was proud of how it had gone. A few days later, I was in the middle of doing something when I realized I had forgotten to be scared during the interview. It was such a great experience that I can't wait to do it again.

As I have developed my daily practice of meditation, journaling, hypnosis, and mini habit shifts, these techniques have changed my emotional response to the tasks and responsibilities ahead of me. Things that used to be very challenging have become things I can easily and comfortably do. It seems so simple now, but it was not so easy and simple when I saw those things only as a huge hill to climb. I now use this as my example when I get overwhelmed at the road ahead. I just break it down to mini shifts that I add to my day. I know that the world is working with me, not against me.

I realized at some point that whatever I focus on in terms of emotions and perceptions is what I am programming into my brain. There were thoughts that were on autopilot, ones that did not work for me. They used to show up at night and disturbed my sleep. I had to consciously decide to not allow them to run my life anymore. I pictured the human body: It could either choose to stand or to sit. It could not, however, do them both at the same time.

One can't have positive thoughts and negative thoughts at the same time. When I started to go down a rabbit hole, I would stop myself instantly and focus on the positive. I started saying the same prayer over and over again. I knew that would keep my brain busy; it works for me.

I began writing a gratitude list that I would repeat until I fell asleep. Incredibly, I don't have to do that anymore. Now, if I wake up in the middle of the night, I just meditate. Next thing I know, it is morning and I realized I had fallen asleep. More importantly, the last information my conscious brain received before it shut down was positivity, allowing my subconscious mind to run on that program all night and into the day ahead.

I now control my thoughts and point them in the direction I want my life to go. My thoughts serve me, instead of me being a servant to my thoughts.

LOUISA JOVANOVICH

About Louisa Jovanovich: Louisa is the founder of Connect with Source. She is a mindfulness and emotional intelligence coach. She helps identify blindspots and create new beliefs which empower her clients to access a life they have never dreamed possible. She has completed twenty years of personal and transformational growth including Landmark Forum, Gratitude Training, and is a Clarity Catalyst Certified Trainer. She works with entrepreneurs who seek clarity and want to up-level their lives.

Her life experiences and school of hard knocks are what make her a knowledgeable and compassionate leader and enable her to help guide others through the process of looking for answers within in order to find success and breakthrough their limiting beliefs. Her unique coaching techniques help her clients see the truth behind the stories that are keeping them stuck in the reality that they created.

Louisa is a single mother of two teenagers living in LA. Her love and compassion towards others are her superpowers, helping others reclaim their confidence, find their voice, and know their worth.

Author's Website: *www.ConnectWithSource.com*

Book Series Website: *www.The13StepsToRiches.com*

Lynda Sunshine West

WHAT WE DON'T SEE CAN HURT US

"Everything which man creates BEGINS in the form of a thought impulse."
~ **Napoleon Hill**

Imagine, if you will, 365 days in a row doing something that will forever change your life. What could that possibility be? If you were to do this one thing every day for an entire year, your life will change dramatically. I guarantee it.

January 1, 2015, I woke up and had an epiphany. I was fifty-one years old and realized that I had allowed fear to control my entire life—all fifty-one years.

So, what would I choose to do about it? Why would I want to do anything? Why not just live my Groundhog Day life for the rest of my life?

Something inside of me told me that I didn't want to continue down the same path. I decided to do something new, something I never thought of before, something that would change my life forever. It put me on a trajectory of which I never could have consciously been aware.

I decided in that moment, without prior thought (consciously at least), what I was going to do. I knew I wanted something different out of life and that's when it started: I had an idea that if I break through one fear every single day, 365 days in a row, that my life *might* change. And boy did it!

Here's what that year looked like: Every single morning when I woke up, before I got out of bed, I asked myself one simple question. This one question would shape the rest of my life. This one question would help me to move into faith over fear at the drop of a hat. This one simple question would create within my subconscious and conscious mind something that would help me to step into who I was born to be. It was the most incredible year of my life, and I'm so glad I did it.

The question I asked myself every day for 365 days was, "What scares me?"

Yep, those simple three words changed my life.

After I asked that question, I would lay in bed and I would wait until the very first fear popped into my head. My commitment to myself was that every day I would break through the fear that popped into my head no matter what. I couldn't add up the fears day by day, but had to break through it THAT day. I had no idea what results I would get from this journey, but I knew I had so many fears and needed to do something different in order to live a different life.

You see, I grew up in a very volatile, abusive, alcoholic household where fear was the controlling factor of everything I did. I lived my life riddled with fear.

When I was five years old, I decided to run away and was gone for a whole week. I just went to the neighbor's house, and I was safe, but for all intents and purposes, I was going to be gone forever (at least in my mind). My mom brought me back home after a week, and that is when fear started to settle in me so deeply that it would control my every move.

In 2015, when I decided to break through one fear a day, I was fifty-one years old. It was the greatest gift I've ever given to myself.

This chapter is about the subconscious mind, and I want to share with you how I see my Year of Fears playing into the subconscious mind, already working on the fear while I was asleep. This is my own belief and there is no science that I know of to prove my theory. Since the subconscious mind is working twenty-four hours a day, seven days a week, it stands to reason that this is what was happening.

While I was sleeping, my brain knew I was going to ask the question in the morning, and it came up with an answer to my question, "What scares me?" My subconscious was on hyperdrive figuring out what fear I needed to break through that day.

About six months into breaking through a fear every day (180 days in a row), I had another epiphany. The vast majority of my fears were based on the fear of judgment, also known as Social Anxiety Disorder. It is an intense, persistent fear of being watched and judged by others.

There's a saying that, "More people are scared of speaking on stage than they are of dying." I don't agree with that at all. The reality is that more people are scared of the judgment they will receive from speaking on stage than they are of dying. If we rid ourselves of the fear of judgment, our lives will forever be changed.

One of the greatest things that happened to me during that year is that my fear of judgment pretty much disappeared, and it no longer controls me. That is a huge shift.

The most common question I get asked about breaking through a fear every day is, "Were they the same fears every single day or were they different?" All of my fears were different, yet some were very similar. You see, the fear of judgment shows up in many ways in our lives, including, but not limited to, procrastination, perfectionism, not being good enough, failure, disappointing others, etc. When we rid ourselves of the fear of judgment, we rid ourselves of perfection syndrome and show up 100% of the time as ourselves.

My belief is that the fear of judgment is what creates a lot of negativity in this world. You see judgment all over the place because we're human, and humans are judgmental beings. However, the judgment of others only has a hold over us if we allow it.

I urge you to take a look at your life and think about the fears that you have and then look at those fears to recognize what is the underlying current of what is causing that fear. If you find it to be the fear of judgment, you just won the prize because now you can work on overcoming your fear of judgment. Yes, it is possible. Yes, I have done it, and living my life without fear of judgment has freed me to be me everywhere I am.

LYNDA SUNSHINE WEST

About Lynda Sunshine West: As the Founder and CEO of Action Takers Publishing, Lynda Sunshine West's mission is to empower five million women and men to share their stories with the world to make a greater impact on the planet. She is affectionately known as The Queen of Collaboration.

Lynda Sunshine is a Book Publisher, Speaker, Multiple Times #1 International Bestselling Author, Executive Film Producer, and a Red Carpet Interviewer. At the age of five, she ran away and was gone an entire week. She came home riddled with fears that stopped her from living and, in turn, became a people-pleaser.

At age fifty-one, she decided to face one fear every day for an entire year. In doing so, she gained an exorbitant amount of confidence and now uses what she learned to fulfill her mission. She believes in cooperation and collaboration and loves connecting with like-minded people.

Author's Website: *www.ActionTakersPublishing.com*

Book Series Website: *www.The13StepstoRiches.com*

Maris Segal & Ken Ashby

YOU ARE THE CEO OF SUBCON

Through a complex mechanism of neurological functions, our brains are responsible for vital emotions, both positive and negative. These include anger, happiness, grief, joy, shock, wonderment, and awe. These interpretations give shape to the kind of behavior we exhibit. It influences whether a person cultivates positive thinking or limiting beliefs. This is SubCon!

Imagine for a moment a boardroom, well-appointed with a large oval-shaped table, handcrafted from the finest wood available. The table is surrounded by elegant leather chairs, all neatly organized and seemingly guarding the shiny oval surface. This boardroom is the proud centerpiece of the *SubCon* organization. In this space, *SubCon* has the capabilities to cultivate many brilliant ideas that bring the owner's vision—your vision —into reality. *SubCon* is made up of individual owners, like you and me, who seek and receive input and stimulus on a regular basis. The performance of *SubCon* is dependent on the leadership of its individual owners.

SubCon, metaphorically, represents every human's **subcon**scious mind. The subconscious mind is the "autopilot" behind our conscious mind. It is where our mind files away all memories, keeps our experiences, concepts, insights, and perceptions long after our conscious mind has forgotten them. From here come the positive or negative feelings and notions that rule our conscious self, behaviors, habits, and decision-making. Our *SubCon* is engaged and informs everything we consider and/or are "doing" consciously.

We Have a Choice

From our youth into our adulthood, our cherished memories, our dramas, and our traumas seed our *SubCon*. These experiences influence our conscious behaviors in both our personal and professional lives and open the door to our choices in how we react and/or respond to them. We are the *SubCon* owners and its CEO. We can either choose joy, celebration, connection, and empowerment, or we can choose anger, fear, and disconnection. However, our subconscious is programmable toward either negative or positive words with ourselves and others.

As the story continues, *SubCon's* market penetration is omnipresent and is without argument a resident system that lives inside each of us. Our *SubCon* makes up 95% of brain power and handles everything our body needs from eating and breathing to memories. *SubCon* communicates with the conscious mind to drive our actions and operates on vibrational frequencies. The higher and more rapid the vibrations are, the wider the door opens to experience the best that life has to offer personally and professionally. The more positive energy we put out, the higher the vibration and greater success in our relationships and our lives. How we feel inside is how we show up everywhere. It is an inside-out job!

"You are the CEO of your *SubCon!*" That means that we are responsible for our personal subconscious, and we perceive a myriad of creative vibrations resonating in everything we do. Our subconscious mind is an infinite stream, a flowing cornucopia of imaginative, inspired, and innovative thoughts just waiting to be plucked off the idea conveyor belt and put into conscious action.

Our subconscious mind is the most powerful support foundation for everything that we think about acting upon. So, what we tell ourselves in our heads shows up in our behaviors. *SubCon* CEOs have long since understood that internal mindset and mind-programming results in a greater advantage for creating success and thriving in all relationships, personal, professional, and with the planet. It's vital in our daily lives to be acutely aware of these subconscious thoughts, and choose how we operate from them.

Ancient writings from wisdom teacher Lao Tzu tell us (paraphrased), "Watch your THOUGHTS, they become your WORDS, your WORDS become your ACTIONS, your ACTIONS become your HABITS, your HABITS become your CHARACTER, your CHARACTER becomes your DESTINY!" Simply stated, we are our thoughts.

Our subconscious takes everything at face value, without judgment, and without constraints. Take, for example, an uplifting mantra you may have repeated from time to time for a boost to your personal emotional mindset: "I am enough." This phrase, when repeated and spoken to our subconscious, shuttles us away from self-doubt and self-sabotage, which are too often based on limiting beliefs born from negative experiences from our past. Think about your own life: Do "limiting beliefs" hold you back? If so, what's the impact on your life?

Reframing Our *SubCon*

After we become aware of the power we have in our subconscious mind, the next step is reprogramming, or what we call "reframing." This is a simple way to guide your subconscious and create a new perspective, a new way to look at experiences and circumstances, a new point-of-view.

The only way to break free from these negative thoughts, which do not serve you and that have been repeated thousands upon thousands of times in your life, is allowing our subconscious mind to explore these old beliefs by recalling the memory and shifting it's meaning into a new supportive perspective. Since the limiting belief has been repeated thousands of times, likewise, reframing these limiting beliefs will take thousands upon thousands of repetitions in order to replace the restrictive thoughts that we have carried for so long. Thoughts that have held us back, kept us stuck, and limited our success personally and professionally.

Remember, when we send programming information to our **subcon**scious, we set in motion a support system that accepts our reframed idea as true and significant. From the moment we reframe and reprogram the limiting thoughts, our subconscious begins working on them and bringing our true vision to fruition. What experiences in your life could benefit from reframing?

"When reframing we lead with gratitude, we accept and meet people where they are, and we honor their feedback as neutral. When we reframe, a different perspective emerges, and a shift can happen!"
~ The *R*Factor.

Our Reframing Reality

We've been living, loving, and working together for almost 20 years. For many years we had played with the idea that we could write a book and about two years ago we began reprogramming our limiting beliefs. Reframing the kind of self-talk that said we had nothing important to write about, that maybe we weren't good enough, etc. None of these limiting thoughts are supportive in doing anything creative. So, we made an audacious declaration that "in six months we would have a number one bestselling book." Mind you, we hadn't yet written a single word.

One morning we woke up and just began writing, and writing, and writing. We developed about 50,000 words and then sent our draft to an editor. The editor wasn't a good fit and we pulled it back and were committed to doing more work on the manuscript and felt a bit defeated. However, remember that declaration of, "a bestselling book in six months," by repeating it over and over, morning and night, our subconscious kept working on the "truth" we had declared.

Then one day we received an invitation to write in this collaborative series, *The 13 Steps to Riches*. We said yes and began writing and submitting chapters. On the day before the end of our six-month declaration we received notification that our first coauthored book was, in fact, a number one bestseller and we were invited to a book signing at one of the largest book retailers in the country! That's the power of SubCon! What declarations will you feed your **subcon**scious?

The Next Step in Human Evolution

During our work as executive producers, business consultants, coaches, and mentors, we saw a pattern in the people we were engaged with. We began to notice a one common factor that seems to hold so many people back is a pervasive feeling of "not being enough." Could it be that we are all here, in this one body, one life, one planet to understand that actually, "we are enough?" The key is in the *purposeful action to reprogram and reframe our subconscious mind.*

Recognition and awareness of our innate ability to be in control of our mind by reprogramming our subconscious thoughts is also a sign of our divinity. Author and theologian Richard Rohr calls this "the face you had before you were born." This childlike acceptance of our true self and our relationship with our subconscious creates the possibility of being the CEO of our own lives and taking ownership of our own SubCon!

Tapping into the strength of our subconscious is undoubtedly the single most important step we can make in bringing our vision to reality. We have an opportunity to let go of self-doubt, self-beat-up, and judging ourselves by taking ownership of and reframing our own SubCon. This act of reframing is choosing to lead in a no-judgment-zone and involves a childlike approach, being curious, being playful, taking empowered action, and knowing that this human possibility is available to each of us, 24/7!

Reframing our SubCon is not passive; it's an active investment, and the next step in owning your SubCon. Reframing your SubCon is a leadership opportunity which depends solely on you, its CEO! The ROI of reframing our SubCon may be a significant step in human evolution.

MARIS SEGAL & KEN ASHBY

About Ken Ashby & Maris Segal: From Mindset to Marketing, Ken Ashby and Maris Segal, a husband and wife dynamic duo, have spent the last thirty-plus years bringing an innovative, collaborative voice to issues, causes, and brands. As entrepreneurs, activists, business strategists, executive producers, coaches, authors, speakers, and trainers, Ken and Maris work with the public and private sectors from boardrooms and classrooms to the world stage. They are known for creating high touch experiences that unite diverse populations across a broad spectrum of business, policy, and social issues.

Their leadership expertise in Business Relationship Marketing, Organizational Change and Cultural Inclusion, Personal Growth, Project Management, Public Affairs, and Philanthropy Strategies has been called upon by companies and their agencies. Their experience includes consumer and financial brands, Olympic organizers, Super Bowls, America's 400th Anniversary, Harvard Kennedy School, Archdiocese of LA and NY Papal visit planners, the White House, and celebrities across the arts, entertainment, sports, and culinary genres. With Ken's expertise as an award-winning singer-songwriter, they launched ONE SONG, a songwriting workshop series designed to unleash creativity in individuals and teams.

Their **DRIVE** method: **D**esire, **R**elationships, **I**ntention, **V**ision and **E**mpowerment sits at the core of their companies Prosody Creative Services, ONE SONG, and Segal Leadership Global to set a path for every client to Build High Performing Businesses and Elevate Personal and Professional Leadership for Maximum Impact and a 360-degree Thriving Life!

Author's Website: *www.SegalLeadershipGlobal.com*

Book Series Website: *www.The13StepsToRiches.com*

Mel Mason

THE HIDDEN FILES: HOW SUBCONSCIOUS PROGRAMMING GOVERNS OUR BEHAVIOR

When someone struggles to make a change in their life, it is often because they have neglected to access the power force behind their actions: the subconscious mind. In *Think and Grow Rich*, Napoleon Hill considers the subconscious mind "the connecting link between the finite mind of man and infinite intelligence." If a person does not do the self-work to become aware of what's happening in their subconscious mind, it will be difficult to create lasting change in their life.

The subconscious mind is what lies beneath our actions, behaviors, and the conscious mind. The subconscious mind is always working even if the conscious mind is not. We can think of the subconscious mind like the programming on a computer. The program running in the background (our subconscious) determines how we consciously function. When a person quits smoking, but returns to the habit three weeks later, it's not that they consciously chose to pick up smoking again. Instead, they returned to the habit because they didn't address the subconscious programming underneath the conscious smoking habit.

We are not born into the world with programming, though. We come into the world with an empty hard-drive, and from birth to around eight years old our hard-drive fills up with software and programming. Our experiences and messages, both implicit and explicit, determine what sorts of programs we internalize. Because this programming is informed by unique experiences, everyone has different subconscious mind software. One person might be able to quit smoking and never look back. Others will fight a battle with quitting their whole life (or at least until they address the programming in their subconscious mind that makes smoking habitual).

Examples of unique subconscious programming are all around us. Two people facing the same situation will interpret it in opposite ways based on their programming. Consider the grocery store clerk. Only one customer asks them how they are doing their whole shift. So, they go home and complain to their partner about the customers' indifferent behavior. Another clerk goes home and gushes to their partner about the one kind customer who they spoke with at work.

The situation is the same, yet it reveals two different subconscious programs. One person has the subconscious programming to focus on the negatives of the day (all the customers who did not say hello). The other has the subconscious programming to look upon the one interaction during the day as a positive, which outshines the drearier components of the day.

The programming we receive as children tends to influence us the most, but our subconscious mind can also be impacted by events and messages we receive as adolescents and adults. A resilient child might turn into a fearful young adult after years of bullying in high school. A demure woman might find new strength after surviving a mugging. A queer queen might embrace their unique identities upon finding a community where they feel accepted.

Because the subconscious largely operates in the background, it is often difficult to notice our own programming. Most of us don't realize the effect of our subconscious mind until we are faced with unwanted results. In my coaching practice, clients come to me when they need help sorting through their clutter—their faulty or outdated programming has manifested in an unwanted result of external mess. Then, the work I do with clients doesn't target the clutter, but rather the client's subconscious programming. Unless I help them address their subconscious programming, the clutter will only return once their home is cleaned. Unwanted outcomes mean it is time to reprogram.

Once someone has identified that they have results they don't want, the first step toward reprogramming is to become aware of the faulty programming. But awareness is always a process. In 2019, I did intense self-work, and it paid off. In 2020, I had the best year of business to date, connecting with more clients and closing more leads than ever before. I was married, in great health, and at the top of my career success in a year where many people had to put their life on pause.

But then in 2021, my life fell apart. I struggled to close any leads and I started self-sabotaging. I divorced, I drove too fast, I drank, and I picked up a nasty smoking habit. For some reason, my subconscious programming had me self-sabotaging in every area of my life.

What was happening? While I had updated some outdated subconscious programming in 2019, the challenges and situations the following two years revealed a new faulty subconscious program.

When we are faced with unwanted results, the first step toward change is to become aware of the subconscious programming governing our conscious behavior. When I was finally willing to look, I saw that all of my unwanted results in 2021 arose because I had subconscious programming that said, "*If my brother didn't get to live and be successful, why should I?*"

The awareness of my subconscious programming was the steppingstone to change. I increased my awareness of how this program determined much of my behavior. When I was in a challenging situation where I desired new results, I brought my subconscious program to conscious attention. With awareness of the limiting belief, my actions slowly became a matter of conscious choice. As I gained awareness, I could then choose a different action and belief. Overtime, I rewrote the subconscious programming about my worth.

The more we become aware of the subconscious programming, the better equipped we are to change it. We can pause in a moment of strife or stress and be aware of the programming operating in the background. The programming may nudge us to behave in a certain way. Maybe we shy away from interacting with the cute stranger at the coffee bar. Maybe we rant like a child when we don't receive the promotion we wanted. Maybe every stressor feels overwhelming and so we run away and lock ourselves in the bathroom to avoid it. All of these behaviors can be interrupted (and eventually resisted) if we cultivate awareness of the subconscious program operating underneath.

Similar to how our electronics operate, we can't update our subconscious programming once and expect it to work correctly for the rest of our lives. Like a computer, our programming needs regular updating. We can clear out old files and programs we aren't using any more to make space for new ones.

However, even when we have become aware of faulty programming and deleted the files slowing us down, we might still create unwanted results. Maybe we start closing more deals, but we can't seem to close the big deal which would allow us to attain financial security for the year. In these scenarios, we have likely forgotten to check our hidden files.

I often record my climbs and transfer the video from camera to computer using an SD card. As soon as I download the footage, I delete the files on the SD card to make space for more video. But after a few months of use, the SD card registered in my camera as "full."

I complained to a rock-climbing buddy at the gym, and he asked me, "Did you delete them from the hidden folder too?"

"What do you mean?" I asked.

"Well," he said, chalking his hands, "usually even if you delete data from the card, it stores a back-up in a hidden folder. You need to delete those too for full capacity."

In this conversation, I had two revelations. The first was how to fix my SD card problem. The second (and arguably more profound) was about the hidden files in our subconscious mind. Even when we think we've reprogrammed our subconscious, hidden files keep us struggling. If we're still receiving unwanted outcomes, it's not necessarily because we didn't reprogram correctly. Likely, there are hidden files operating which need addressing.

The hidden files are akin to the upper limit problem (which Gay Hendricks covers in his book *The Big Leap*). We might close business leads that provide stability for a few months at a time, but a hidden file is interfering with our programming. The file might determine that we can be successful in bursts, but not in the long-term. We might have an upper limit which says we can make $80,000 in a year, but not more than that. So, we fail to close easy long-term deals without knowing why. Hidden files and upper limits cap our capacity for joy, abundance, and all that is good—when, in reality, desired results can be limitless.

The subconscious mind is a vast network of files and programs governing our actions. It can feel overwhelming to poke around and discover what beliefs are influencing our conscious choices. But the wonderful news is that we can voluntarily reprogram, delete, and install the software in the subconscious mind—it does not have to be an involuntary process. And through cultivating a practice of allowing the now and continually looking at results, even hidden folders can be cleared, making space in our lives for more joy, abundance, and all that is wanted.

MEL MASON

About Mel Mason: International Bestselling Author Mel Mason is The Clutter Expert, and as a sexual abuse survivor, she grew up depressed, suicidal, and surrounded by clutter. What she realized after coming back from the brink of despair and getting through her own chaos was that the outside is just a mirror of the inside, and if you only address the outside without changing the inside, the clutter keeps coming back.

That set her on a mission to empower people around the world to get free from clutter inside and out, so they can experience happiness and abundance in every area of their lives.

She is the author of *Freedom from Clutter: The Guaranteed, Foolproof, Step-by-Step Process to Remove the Stuff That's Weighing You Down.*

Author's Website: *www.FreeGiftFromMel.com*

Book Series Website: *www.The13StepsToRiches.com*

Dr. Miatta Hampton

PLAN, DESIRE, PURPOSE

*"You cannot entirely control your
subconscious mind, but you can voluntarily
hand over to it any plan, desire, or purpose
which you wish transformed
into concrete
form."*
~ Napoleon Hill

MIATTA HAMPTON

About Dr. Miatta Hampton: Dr. Miatta Hampton is a nurse leader, #1 Bestselling Author, speaker, coach, and minister. Miatta impacts others with her powerful, relatable messages of pursuing purpose, and she empowers her audiences to live life on purpose and according to their dreams. She coaches and inspires women to turn chaos into cozy, pivot to prosperity, and how to profit in adversity. Miatta provides tools and resources for personal, professional, and financial growth.

Author's Website: *www.DrMiattaSpeaks.com*

Book Series Website: *www.The13StepsToRiches.com*

Michael D. Butler

UNLEASHING THE POWER OF THE SUBCONSCIOUS MIND: A DIVINE CONNECTION

In the past decade, the discourse surrounding the subconscious mind has undergone a profound shift, evolving from a niche topic in esoteric circles to a mainstream conversation about personal and professional development. Napoleon Hill's timeless work, *Think and Grow Rich*, has been instrumental in bridging this gap, inviting individuals from diverse backgrounds to explore the practical dimensions of the subconscious mind.

As an ordained Pastor, my perspective aligns this power with our divine connection, framing the subconscious mind as the inner voice that guides us. In this chapter, we will delve into the practical aspects of developing this innate power, spotlighting moments of quiet reflection, intuitive listening, and spiritual focus. Real-world illustrations will illuminate how this divine connection empowers a mother raising children, an entrepreneur scaling a business, and a young innovator shaping the future of technology.

The Quietude of Motherhood

Amidst the whirlwind of daily life, mothers raising children often find solace in the quiet moments that punctuate their days. This tranquility becomes a conduit to the subconscious mind, offering insights and guidance in the intricate dance of parenting. Through intentional reflection, a mother can discern the subtle nuances of her children's needs, transforming the chaotic symphony of motherhood into a harmonious melody.

Picture a mother, surrounded by the clamor of household chores and the laughter of playing children. Sensing the need for a moment of stillness, she retreats to a quiet corner for a brief meditation. In the tranquility of that space, her subconscious mind guides her to implement a creative and educational playtime routine. This simple shift not only enriches her children's lives but also strengthens the bond between mother and child.

The Entrepreneur's Spiritual Focus

Entrepreneurs navigate a bustling landscape where decisions can shape the trajectory of their businesses. By turning inward and cultivating a spirit-focused approach, they align their entrepreneurial journey with a deeper purpose. The subconscious mind, acting as a strategic ally, provides clarity amidst uncertainty, enabling business leaders to make decisions that resonate with their values and drive sustainable growth.

Imagine an entrepreneur at a crossroads, contemplating the expansion of their company. Amidst the noise of market trends and financial projections, the entrepreneur decides to embark on a weekend retreat for spiritual reflection. In the silence of this retreat, the subconscious mind becomes a guiding light, leading the entrepreneur to a decision that not only enhances profitability but also fosters a workplace culture rooted in integrity and purpose.

The Innovator's Quest

In the dynamic realm of innovation, a young college student is on a mission to revolutionize the tech industry. Driven by a desire to create a software solution that saves both time and money, this innovator understands that the subconscious mind is a wellspring of creativity and problem-solving. Through intentional practices of listening and reflection, the student taps into this well of inspiration, guiding the development of a groundbreaking solution to real-world problems.

Envision a college student immersed in the world of algorithms and code, seeking to address inefficiencies in business operations. By incorporating mindfulness practices into their routine, the student accesses the power of the subconscious mind, leading to innovative breakthroughs. In a pivotal moment, the solution to a complex problem emerges, laying the foundation for a software platform that transforms industries, saves resources, and propels the student into the ranks of visionary tech leaders.

As the discourse on the subconscious mind permeates mainstream awareness, individuals across diverse fields are discovering the transformative power of this divine connection. By embracing moments of quiet reflection, intuitive listening, and spiritual focus, we unlock the latent potential within, transforming our lives and endeavors. Whether navigating the nuances of motherhood, scaling a business, or pioneering innovation, the subconscious mind stands as a guiding force, propelling us toward success, growth, and a harmonious existence.

In the cacophony of modern life, where incessant sales messages and distractions compete for our attention, the true challenge lies in reclaiming the power of the subconscious mind. It's a call to action for individuals across all ages, professions, and walks of life—because the potential within each of us is boundless, waiting to be unleashed.

To embark on this transformative journey, we must courageously confront the noise that surrounds us. In a world that bombards us 24/7, the first step is to unplug, creating space for the quietude necessary to hear the whispers of our subconscious mind. This intentional disconnect from the external chatter allows us to delve deep into our inner thoughts, intuitions, and leadings—the very essence of our divine connection.

As we navigate the labyrinth of our thoughts, we find the seeds of premonitions and insights that can guide us towards profound personal and professional growth. It's not just about listening to the inner voice; it's about putting those revelations into action in our lives and businesses. Whether you're a mother nurturing a family, an entrepreneur steering a company, or an innovator shaping the future, the subconscious mind stands ready to be your guiding force.

In a world enamored with constant stimuli, carving out moments of intentional reflection, intuitive listening, and spiritual focus becomes a revolutionary act. It's a pledge to reclaim your mental space, allowing the profound wisdom of your subconscious mind to shape your decisions, illuminate your path, and elevate your existence.

So, here's the challenge and the invitation: dare to unplug, embrace the quietude, and let the power of your subconscious mind be the driving force in your life. It's time to transcend the noise, defy the distractions, and step into a realm where your inner wisdom reigns supreme. The journey is unique for everyone, but the destination is universal—a life infused with success, growth, and a harmonious existence.

As we embark on this collective awakening, let the power of the subconscious mind propel us beyond the limitations of the ordinary. Join the movement, rise above the noise, and discover the extraordinary potential that resides within you. The world is waiting for the brilliance that only you can bring forth when you unlock the divine connection within your subconscious mind.

MICHAEL D. BUTLER

About Michael D. Butler: Called the Simon Cowell of Book Publishing, celebrity kingmaker Michael D. Butler is most proud of his four sons and two grandsons. His authors have spoken in 50 countries. As a global book publisher and speaker Butler is a recognized authority in the book publishing space with 794 titles published by authors in 64 nations. Helping authors and speakers evolve and create platforms of influence in an ever-changing marketplace.

Founder of 1040Impact.org has rescued 394 girls from human trafficking ages 6-17, caring for them in a safe loving environment with a full-time staff of twenty-five in Pakistan.

Author's Website: *www.MichaelDButler.com*

Book Series Website: *www.The13StepsToRiches.com*

Michelle Cameron Coulter & Al Coulter

AWAKEN YOUR INNER SUPERPOWER

Picture this: Oprah Winfrey holding a washer on a string while Deepak Chopra works his mind-bending magic. He suggests to Oprah that the washer should start moving, and, lo and behold, it obeys his command, swaying back and forth, and even spinning in circles. It's like a real-life Jedi mind trick! What's the secret behind this mind-blowing display? It's the power of the subconscious mind, my friend.

You see, Michelle and I were glued to our seats, watching this mind-boggling episode. It got us thinking about the untapped potential hiding deep within our own minds. And, as luck would have it, I had the perfect testing ground to explore this phenomenon: coaching our four children in volleyball.

Now, coaching volleyball isn't just about perfecting serves and setting skills. It's about diving into the minds of our players and tapping into their subconscious power. So, armed with the knowledge that the subconscious mind is like a sponge, absorbing everything around it, I started implementing some sneaky subconscious coaching techniques.

At the start of each season, I'd gather the team and declare that we were going to be a defensive machine. The other coaches thought I was crazy. "Offense wins games!" they'd say. But I knew better. I understood the hidden potential of our subconscious minds. We started slow, building confidence by nailing those well-placed digs. And every Thursday, we cranked up the intensity, practicing against hard-hitting balls that would make your head spin. By the end of the season, our team had developed a resilience that was unshakeable. Nothing fazed us because we had programmed our minds to believe that we could dig anything that came our way.

But that was just the beginning. I wanted the players to be their own coaches, to rely on each other for support and guidance. So, instead of having one player in the spotlight, we created an atmosphere of collaboration. Multiple drills were happening simultaneously, with everyone actively involved. They didn't even realize that while they were hitting balls at each other, they were also honing their accuracy and touch, and building trust within the team. And boy, did it work! The girls were improving faster than ever before, and they didn't even know why. It was our little secret.

As the season progressed, I made sure to remind the team of their progress and hard work. I'd gather them together, pointing out the countless skills they had developed and the number of ball touches they had achieved. And then I'd drop the bomb: "We're getting more contacts than any other team out there. We're becoming unstoppable!" It was like planting a seed in their subconscious minds, reinforcing their belief in themselves and their abilities.

When the big Provincial Championship rolled around, we were the underdogs. But we had something no other team possessed: a subconscious mind primed for success. We were a force to be reckoned with, driven by unyielding confidence. And guess what? We shocked everyone by winning the tournament. The other teams may have had more talent on paper, but they didn't have the secret weapon of the subconscious mind working for them.

Our journey didn't stop at the volleyball court. Michelle and I carried this newfound understanding of the subconscious mind into our parenting. We created a daily ritual of sharing our highs and lows, focusing on the positive aspects and celebrating our achievements. By doing so, we nurtured an environment where our children's subconscious minds were constantly fed with affirmations of their own brilliance and potential.

It's incredible to think about the power we hold within us. The subconscious mind is like a superpower, waiting to be unleashed. We can shape our destinies and manifest our dreams by tapping into its extraordinary capabilities. It's like having a personal superhero residing within us, ready to spring into action.

And let me tell you, the impact goes beyond the volleyball court and our family life. The principles we discovered are universal. The subconscious mind isn't limited to sports or parenting—it's a game-changer for every aspect of our lives. It's the key to unlocking our true potential and achieving greatness.

Imagine applying this subconscious coaching approach to your career. Instead of doubting your abilities or fearing failure, you can program your mind to believe in your skills and envision your success. With a confident and empowered subconscious mind, you'll be amazed at how you tackle challenges, seize opportunities, and achieve remarkable results.

Or how about in relationships? By feeding your subconscious mind with positive affirmations and visualizations, you can enhance your self-esteem, attract healthy connections, and foster deeper connections with your loved ones. It's like rewiring your mind for love, joy, and fulfillment.

Even in the pursuit of personal goals, the subconscious mind plays a pivotal role. Whether it's losing weight, learning a new skill, or starting a business, programming your subconscious with affirmations and visualizations can make all the difference. It amplifies your focus, resilience, and determination, propelling you towards your desired outcomes.

So, my friend, it's time to tap into your own inner superhero. Dive deep into the power of your subconscious mind. Immerse yourself in the realm of affirmations, visualizations, and positive self-talk. Embrace the potential within you and watch as it transforms your life.

But remember, it's not an overnight miracle. Just like building a strong volleyball team, harnessing the power of the subconscious mind takes time, dedication, and practice. It's a journey of self-discovery and growth. Be patient with yourself, celebrate small victories along the way, and trust in the process.

As you embark on this extraordinary adventure, always remember that the power lies within you. The subconscious mind is your greatest ally, waiting to be awakened and unleashed. Believe in yourself, set your intentions, and let the magic unfold.

So go ahead, my friend. Embrace the power of the subconscious mind. Unleash your inner superpower. And watch as your dreams turn into reality. The journey awaits, and the possibilities are endless.

MICHELLE CAMERON COULTER & AL COULTER

About Michelle Cameron Coulter: Michelle is an Olympic gold medalist, entrepreneur, mother of four, community leader raising millions of dollars for charities, global inspirational leader, and founder and CEO of Inspiring Possibilities.

About Al Coulter: Al is a two-time Olympian in volleyball, captain of Team Canada, world record holder in matches representing one's country in any sport, with over 735 matches, entrepreneur, father of four, and personal best coach, specializing in relationships, team, and resilience.

Michelle and Al are the embodiment of today's leaders. Strong and empowering, they embraced life's challenges with strength and courage. They bring insight, compassion, depth, and inspiration to the table with multiple world championships, three Olympics, an Olympic gold medal, marriage, and four children.

They are sought-after inspirational leaders. Through their speaking, workshops, and retreats, their gift and passion is to "inspire possibilities" and encourage people to embrace their greatness in a real, authentic, healthy, and vibrant way—creating thriving community, connection, and one's own gold medal results.

Author's Website: *www.MichelleCameronCoulter.com*

Book Series Website: *www.The13StepsToRiches.com*

Dr. Michelle Mras

STAR IT

When something is important, you must tell yourself, "Important/star it," so your brain will mark it for easy access when you need it.

Are you aware of the immense capacity we hold within us, particularly in the space between our ears? It's been calculated that the conscious mind processes approximately forty bits of information per second. The subconscious mind can process 20,000,000 bits of information per second. We interact with the world with our conscious mind. We see a tree and think, "Oh, it's a tree." Then we determine what type of tree it is or whatnot.

All the while, our subconscious mind is running through millions of bytes of data about the tree, i.e., height in relation to everything around the tree, species of trees we've seen before, the color of the trunk, along with the texture and pattern of that trunk.

Simultaneously, our subconscious is also calculating the multiple color variations of every leaf of that tree and the fluttering of each, whether an animal is in the tree or if a bird is flying by and at what rate the clouds are passing in relation to the angle in which the sunlight is reflecting upon the tree.

The next time you look at a tree, realize how much data your subconscious is really taking in. By the way, once you start assessing what your subconscious is taking in, the very thought causes a billion other data points for your subconscious to intake. The idea of thinking causing more thinking makes me smile.

It brings to my mind (if we want to get very specific—the thought triggered my subconscious mind to remember) a scene from the movie, *Monty Python and the Holy Grail*. In it, one group is trying to tell another not to say a particular (albeit, common) word because it causes them great pain. When the offending group asks, "What word?" the first group keeps inadvertently saying it while trying not to, thus causing themselves harm. It's quite humorous to understand that what we focus on is what we bring about. Both groups were wanting to avoid the word but could not avoid it.

What do you not want to focus on? By saying you do not what to focus on it, all you do is continue to focus on what you don't want. It happens all the time. Focus on what you want, not what you don't want.

The immense capacity of the subconscious mind sounds like something out of a science fiction movie. Our brain has almost unlimited storage, but most of us have no idea of how to access it. Highly successful thought leaders have shared for generations that we must control the thoughts that enter our minds. The masters suggest that we can develop the skill to input intentionally and train our minds to retrieve what we need at will.

We've discussed the prior concepts of the 13 Steps to Riches: Desire, Faith, Autosuggestion, Specialized Knowledge, Imagination, Organized Planning, Decision, Persistence, Mastermind, and Transmutation. Each step requires the subconscious mind to be the big player to activate each of the other steps.

The subconscious mind is the server mechanism that auto-processes all experiences in our lives. There is nothing that we have sensed, whether it is seen, heard, smelled, tasted, or touched, that hasn't been registered in the subconscious mind.

"The conscious mind is the editor, and the subconscious minds, the writer."
~ Steve Martin

I personally learned the power of our subconscious mind in 2014. I was involved in an auto accident that rendered me unable to move without assistance for over two years. I had obtained a traumatic injury to four areas of my brain. When I began my brain therapies, it became critical for me not to cloud my mind with negativity, violence, or anything that would cause my subconscious mind to process useless or harmful data.

We discovered, during my recovery, that if I watched a high-stress or anxiety-filled movie or listened to aggressive music, my thoughts, emotions, and actions were more aggressive, and I became more agitated. Watching nature videos and listening to ballads or classical music created a less agitated and happier me. Granted, I did not recognize the correlation. My family noticed and commented on what brought the best and worst out of me.

During that time, I had a sixteen-second memory. I was told by my husband that it was as if he was married to the girl from the movie *50 First Dates* with Drew Barrymore. I had no recollection of the day prior. Every day was a new day for me. Slowly, I made progress with my cognition and recognition of people, places, and activities. My family was slowly and methodically creating new memories in my subconscious mind.

The brain damage I had obtained presented a challenge and an opportunity. The challenge was that I lost most of my past experiences. The opportunity was to focus on creating new, pleasant memories in a fertile mind for growth.

The opportunity for growth was ideal. I listened to self-help lectures, joined the John Maxwell Team to hone my leadership skills, and met my mentor in the field of neuroscience and neuroplasticity, Dr. Paul Scheele. I became highly aware of my ability to absorb information and internalize it quickly.

It was as if the clutter within my subconscious mind was absent, and all the new behavior was readily accepted. I planted new belief systems, shed any of the past beliefs that would pop into my scattered memory, and reevaluate whether I wanted any of my old beliefs back. I chose what I allowed in.

With the auto accident and my four areas of traumatic brain injury, I was provided the biggest gift of all... a chance to start anew. This is why I have taken it upon myself to help others through their mental shifts into positivity. I have battled negative thoughts while locked inside my mind for over two years and for several years afterward as I was regrowing neuro-pathways in my mind.

A few years into my recovery, I realized that the old thoughts of inadequacy where still in my mind. I simply chose to not let them materialize in my world or in my actions. Those negative thoughts did not serve the woman I visualized in the future. So, I let them go.

"Whatever we plant in our subconscious mind and nourish with repetition and emotion will one day become a reality."
~ Earl Nightingale

What you allow to remain in your subconscious will reveal itself in your conscious mind. I learned the direct way. There were days I would hear someone say, "Wow! You are doing so well. If I was going through what you have, I would be laying in the dark unable to move." Seriously, the next day, I would have a horrible headache, sit in the dark, and not want to move. My mind would add flair like nausea and vertigo.

I let other people's thoughts invade my thoughts...my subconscious mind. We are that easily swayed even when we don't want to be swayed. That is why we must protect what our conscious mind is exposed to, so that we can protect our prized asset: our subconscious mind.

There's a quote about how you are the sum of the seven people you spend the most time with. It's not just the people. It also applies to what music or visuals you allow into your mind. Our subconscious is always learning. Let it learn and store the data that will build your character, create harmony in your world, and help you develop into the best version of yourself every day.

"My mission in life is not merely to survive, but to thrive and to do so with some, passion, some compassion, some humor and some style."
~ Maya Angelou

What do you want for your future? What thought processes do you have set on auto-play within your subconscious mind? Clean them up. Put what you want in order. Now, feed your mind your mantras, positive affirmations, and prayers daily. Then, watch your world change for the better. What you focus on is what you draw toward yourself. Be sure to tell your brain "Important/star it," and watch what you want come to you.

MICHELLE MRAS

About Michelle Mras, PhD: Michelle is a Global Award-Winning Keynote and TEDx Speaker, Presentation Coach, and co-host of two podcasts: *Denim & Pearls* and Amplifluence. Michelle is the Host of *MentalShift* on The New Channel (TNC), in the Philippines. She's a multiple Bestselling Author and Co-Founder of Amplifuence, amplifying the influence of coaches, authors, and speakers.

Michelle is a survivor of multiple life challenges, including a Traumatic Brain Injury and Breast Cancer. She guides others to recognize the innate gifts within them, stop apologizing for what they are not, and step into who they truly are… unapologetically.

Author's Website: *www.MichelleMras.com*

Book Series Website: *www.The13StepsToRiches.com*

Mickey Stewart

ACT AS IF

"You are a gardener, and you are planting seeds (thoughts) in your subconscious mind all day long, based on your habitual thinking. Your subconscious mind may be likened to the soil, which will grow all kinds of seeds, good or bad. Every thought is, therefore, a cause, and every condition is an effect."
~ Dr. Joseph Murphy, The Power of the Subconscious Mind

"Stop practicing and come set the table for supper!" Mum's words weren't uncalled for or unsupportive. She arrived home every day after work to the sound of the snare drum blasting from my bedroom. She needed help around the house and knew I had already been practicing for the last two hours. In her mind, that was more than sufficient, but for me, it wasn't enough.

I wanted to be so awesome at drumming that I could taste it. But I didn't have any dreams of making a living at it (because it wasn't a thing you did back then), and I didn't know where I could go with it. I didn't even know the World Pipe Band Championships existed, but I was practicing *as if* I was preparing for the Drumming Olympics.

Teenager Mickey was on to something. She didn't know why she had a burning desire to drum obsessively, but she listened to those inspired urges and went all in—you know, the desires that make you feel like you're going to crawl out of your skin if it doesn't happen.

Forgive me for switching to the third person here. I have to because, have you ever looked back at cool things you did in life and thought, *"Did I really do that? Was that actually me?"* Well, that's how I feel thinking about thirteen-year-old Mickey. She was a freakin' badass, and I am in awe of and inspired by her. That's cool, right? To be inspired by yourself?

Teenager Mickey lived by most of Napoleon Hill's principles from *Think and Grow Rich*. She was following her burning desire and trusting with faith that she could do whatever she set her mind to and that things would all work out for her. She used autosuggestion to regularly positively pep-talk herself, was acquiring the specialized knowledge needed to fulfill her dreams, and was using her wildly creative imagination to formulate her future life the way she wanted. She was using them all without realizing it, as an unconscious competent. She was *"acting as if"* she was already the person she wanted to be, planting the seeds Dr. Joseph Murphy refers to above.

Ten years later…

In July 1995, I was on tour with Scotland's Vale of Atholl Pipe Band in Quimper, Brittany, on the west coast of France. The Festival de Cornouaille had us busy with lots of performances, and one event was a solo competition between us (five snare drummers from Scotland) and five snare drummers from Brittany. "You have to play a March, Strathspey & Reel (MSR), and then a French Dance," someone said. "Um, wait now—WHAT? A French Dance? What is that?" I asked one of the other drummers in my band. "I don't know, but someone said it's in Reel time."

After playing my Scottish MSR set, it was time for the French part. As I started my two intro rolls and my not-yet husband, Mark, struck up his bagpipes, my heart pounded with fear at the realization that I had NO IDEA WHAT TO PLAY! In the last split second, I gave myself a firm talking to, "This is what you practiced for all those years. You get to show you're just as good, if not BETTER than some of these guys. Mark is playing for you—he's steady as a rock. He's got you," and some variation of, "Oh, what the heck, go for it anyway."

This tune could have gone very badly, but my "act as if" attitude kicked into overdrive. My sticks started moving as if controlled by an outside force, and it was like I was having an out-of-body experience. It was as if I was witnessing the performance as one of the crowded spectators sitting at our feet in the courtyard of the French castle.

When it came time for prize-giving, I was pleased to be in the top five of not only the MSR, but I somehow managed to beat some of the French drummers at the French Dance. How the heck did that happen? I was literally making it up as I went along, all the while silently having what felt like a minor stroke.

The audience seemed to cheer louder for me than my male counterparts as I went up to get my MSR prize. They were even more boisterous as I received my French Dance prize. I was the only female drummer out of the ten competitors, but there was also a Prix "Special" Féminin, and once again, my new friends went extra with their applause.

I realized it was not only because I was a female beating the men but because they announced me as Michelle Pero (my given maiden name), a very French name, so they saw me proudly as one of them. Parading down the street shortly afterwards, I heard, "GO MICHELLE!" in very thick French accents and looked over to see people from my new "fan club" fist-pumping the air for me.

My teenage self didn't know what I was practicing for, but I had a strong BELIEF that it would pay off someday. It was a fact in my mind. However, I didn't know I would go on to play under the direction of a Five-Time World Drum Corps Champion or find myself holding my own in the courtyard of a French castle against some of the best drummers in the world. I didn't know I would have a successful career where I got paid to drum every day.

I hope my story demonstrates that when you plant "good seeds" and "act as if," your subconscious mind can create an even bigger dream than you could have ever imagined.

Tips for Making Your Subconscious Mind Your BFF:

- Be very mindful of the words you use to talk to yourself and others because every seed you plant will grow.

- Think of your subconscious mind as if it's Sheldon from *The Big Bang Theory*. It can't take a joke and takes everything you tell it literally.

- Use belief, expectation, and assumption as fertilizer for your seeds of thought.

- Listen to your longings and keep acting towards them even if you don't understand why they are important or how they will appear.

- When negative thoughts try to get past the gate from the conscious to the subconscious, you can stop them in their tracks by saying, "Get out of here!"

- Act as if you are already the person you want to be.

You can nurture a seed of passion for years without any evidence of it coming to fruition. Have faith. An acorn does not turn into a mighty oak tree overnight. Little did I know the tiny seed I planted in my teenage bedroom would blossom into a full-blown orchard of opportunities.

MICKEY STEWART

About Mickey Stewart: Born in Cape Breton, Canada, Mickey Stewart is a musician, coach, and author who has been a player and instructor of the snare drum and bodhrán for forty years.

Responsible for heading up the drum program at Ardvreck School in Perthshire, Scotland, since 2002, Mickey is in high demand to teach throughout the U.K. and North America.

Creator and founder of BodhránExpert.com, her YouTube videos have received more than two million views from students and fans from every country throughout the world.

Over the past eight years, she's been involved in the TV and film industry as a supporting artist. Even more recently, she's begun following her newest passion, which is teaching others how to share their talents with the world.

Stewart lives in Crieff, Scotland with her husband of twenty-six years, Scottish musician and composer Mark Stewart, along with their eighteen-year-old son, Cameron, who is also a piper.

Author's Website: *www.MickeyStewart.com*

Book Series Website: *www.The13StepsToRiches.com*

Natalie Susi

THE MAGIC OF THE SUBCONSCIOUS MIND

In his book, *Think and Grow Rich*, Napoleon Hill explores the concept of the subconscious mind and its role in achieving success and prosperity. According to Hill, the subconscious mind is a powerful tool that can be used to achieve our goals and desires but to harness its power; we must first understand its nature and how it works.

The subconscious mind is the part of the mind that operates below the level of conscious awareness. It is responsible for storing and processing information that is not immediately relevant to our current thoughts and actions. The subconscious mind is always working, even when we are not aware of it, and it is responsible for our habits, both good and bad. It is also the source of our beliefs and attitudes, which shape our reality.

One of the key principles of the subconscious mind is that it does not distinguish between positive and negative thoughts. This means that whatever thoughts and beliefs we feed into it, it will take as true and will act upon them. If we constantly think negative thoughts and hold limiting beliefs, the subconscious mind will act upon these and create a negative reality for us. On the other hand, if we feed it with positive thoughts and empowering beliefs, it will act upon those and create a positive reality for us.

To harness the power of the subconscious mind, Hill suggests that we must first become aware of our thoughts and beliefs and then work to change any negative or limiting beliefs that may be holding us back. One way to change our thoughts and beliefs is by using affirmations. Affirmations are positive statements that we repeat to ourselves to change our thinking and beliefs. For example, if we have a belief that we are not good enough, we can use the affirmation "I am good enough" to counter this belief. By repeating this affirmation to ourselves, we can begin to change the way we think and feel about ourselves.

Another way to change our thoughts and beliefs is through visualization. Visualization is the process of creating mental images of what we want to achieve. By visualizing our goals and desires, we can begin to change the way we think and feel about them, and this can help us to take the necessary actions to achieve them. Hill suggests that visualization should be done in a relaxed state, like in meditation, and to be as specific and realistic as possible, including all the five senses in the visualization.

To further access the power of the subconscious mind, Hill suggests using autosuggestion, which is the process of repeatedly suggesting to oneself an idea or goal, which will eventually be accepted by the subconscious and acted upon. This can be done by writing down one's goals and reading them aloud to oneself multiple times a day. The repetition of these suggestions will cause the subconscious mind to accept them as true and will lead to the realization of the goals.

The subconscious mind also plays a role in our emotions and reactions to certain situations. Hill suggests that we must learn to control our emotions and reactions, as they can have a powerful effect on our thoughts and beliefs. By learning to control our emotions, we can change the way we think and feel about different situations, and this can help us to achieve our goals and desires. Negative emotions such as fear, anger, and worry can hold us back and prevent us from taking action towards our goals. Hill suggests replacing those negative emotions with positive ones like faith, love, and courage.

In addition to changing negative thoughts and beliefs, Hill also emphasizes the importance of developing a positive attitude. The subconscious mind is highly influenced by our attitudes, and a positive attitude can help to attract positive opportunities and experiences. Hill suggests that you should surround yourself with positive influences and that you should focus on the positive aspects of life rather than dwelling on the negative.

One of the most important lessons that Hill emphasizes in *Think and Grow Rich* is that we must have a burning desire for what we want to achieve. This desire must be so strong that it becomes an obsession, and it must be backed by a definite plan and constant action towards the goal. The subconscious mind will then work towards the realization of that desire.

Hill also highlights the importance of developing a clear understanding of what you want to achieve and being specific in your goals. The subconscious mind can only work effectively when it has a clear understanding of what it is supposed to do. He suggests writing down your goals in a specific and measurable way, and then reading them aloud multiple times a day. This will help to program your subconscious mind towards the attainment of those goals.

Another important aspect of using the subconscious mind effectively is to eliminate any doubts or fears that may be holding you back. The subconscious mind is highly susceptible to negative thoughts and beliefs, and if these thoughts and beliefs are not addressed, they can prevent you from achieving your goals. Hill suggests that you should make a list of any doubts or fears you may have, and then counter them with positive affirmations. By doing this, you can begin to change the way you think and feel about those doubts and fears, and this can help you to overcome them.

The below combines many of the suggestions above in one fill-in-the-blank exercise that will help you to turn negative thoughts into positive ones and create a visualization statement that will help you reprogram your subconscious around what you'd like to achieve in any particular area of your life. This exercise is simple and will probably feel a bit elementary and repetitive, but it does a great job of reframing your intentions into a format that your subconscious can utilize to call in everything you are looking to experience in any area of your life. I do this all the time for myself and with my clients, and the results are magical!

Follow the Instructions Below for the Manifesting Magic Exercise:

- Fill in the blanks below and write your descriptive visualization about what you'd like to manifest in each area (or just one specific area of your life) on a piece of paper.
- Then, write your final version on a white notecard and read it every morning and every night (white notecard is optional, but I prefer these primarily).

1. I intend to create a reality in which **I FEEL** (three emotions that you want to feel)_____ in XYZ area of my life (Example: In the professional area of my life).
2. When I wake up in the morning, **I THINK** (write down the first thought that you'd think about in this area of your life if it looked the way you want to manifest it) _____ (Example: "I am so excited to open my emails and get started with the day.)
3. When I go to bed at night, **I THINK** (same thing here—can be repetitive or a new thought) _____

   (Example: I feel so accomplished and satisfied today.)
4. When I talk about this area of my life, **I often SAY** things like (something that sounds like you and is something you'd be really proud to say out loud or something you'd be so excited to say) _____ (Example: When I was manifesting my relationship, I wrote here, "I manifested the guy on my freaking vision board.") Make it sound like YOU!
5. When **I FEEL** into this area of my life, I feel it in my XYZ part of my body _____ (Example: my heart feels warm and open, I get goosebumps on my arm, my brain feels clear and calm.)
6. Close with this sentence: "In perfect divine timing for the greatest and highest good of all involved. And so it is."

NATALIE SUSI

About Natalie Susi: Natalie has more than fourteen years of experience as a teacher, speaker, entrepreneur, and mentor. Currently, she's a five-year UCSD professor focusing on communications and the Pursuit of Happiness. As an entrepreneur, she founded and grew Bare Organic Mixers beverage company for eight years resulting in an acquisition in 2014.

After selling the company, Natalie combined her educational background as a teacher and her experience as an entrepreneur to provide personal development coaching and consulting to individuals, businesses, and creative entrepreneurs. She developed a program called Conscious Conversations and utilizes a step-by-step process called The Alignment Method to support leaders in cultivating conscious teams and businesses through a process of self-reflection, self-discover, and self-ascension that ultimately increases profits, productivity, and the growth of the individuals, personally and professionally.

Author's Website: *www.NatalieSusi.com*

Book Series Website: *www.The13StepsToRiches.com*

Nita Patel

REPROGRAMMING YOUR SUBCONSCIOUS

Since when did reprogramming the subconscious mind become so hip? It became popular many decades ago in our modern world; however, the eastern world has been practicing it for much longer. The longing to find new and advanced ways to reprogram the subconscious mind has led us to ancient practices performed thousands of years ago, which are now being validated through modern science.

After years of attempting traditional clinical therapy in the western world, people needed to explore result-oriented options. Additionally, traditional therapy wasn't meant to help you eliminate subconscious beliefs that were genetically embedded from generations ago so that you could live your life in freedom and prosperity.

Traditional therapy is where a licensed professional discusses emotional or psychological distress and helps you devise ways to cope. Ancient therapies such as sound therapy have now been validated by science, which has increased their practice in various forms.

A naturopathic doctor will recommend humming or chanting. A meditation guru will recommend moving your brain to alpha or theta levels. Other experts may direct you toward a sound bath. Someone with an extensive YouTube presence will direct you to their binaural beats or sound videos which are recorded at specific megahertz (MHz) for various purposes.

Ultimately, all these methods lead to reprogramming your subconscious mind towards optimal health (mental, physical, and emotional), wealth, harmonious relationships, and inner peace.

While Beyonce might've woken up *Flawless,* it took a large team of designers, directors, hair and make-up artists, producers, and more to make her look *Flawless* in her music video. We're human, and we come with our own character and attitudes. We add to that the minute we're born, primarily until the age of seven, and oftentimes we pick up unwanted beliefs from those around us.

If those around you were not living with an abundant mindset, chances are you probably have subconscious beliefs blocking you from living your best and abundant life. This is why you also need a team of healers, practitioners, coaches, and more to undo all the beliefs and attitudes that are no longer serving you so that you can experience your flawless life with emotional freedom.

It's not just enough to be rich. What if you have twenty million dollars in your bank account right now, but you struggle with constant disagreements with your spouse, kids, or parents, which keeps you in disharmony? Chances are, it will make you physically sick at some point. Living your best and abundant life is about more than just money.

Reprogramming your subconscious mind will help you in every area of your life if you give it the time, patience, and priority it deserves. The human mind is like an onion, and it has layers and layers of information and memories to which beliefs are attached. It's important to be patient as you peel back the layers and uncover stories that no longer serve you.

We've all experienced some form of trauma during our childhood, including beliefs instilled in us that prevent us from living our best life. Fear, doubt, guilt, shame, and unworthiness are all results of trauma. Thinking you're undeserving of something you really want because you were an older sibling who was always looking out for everyone else can impact how you make decisions for yourself as an adult, even if you don't have anyone to care for directly.

It can be something as simple as a classmate who took your favorite pencil by accident, and it made you feel like you lost something significant, which translates to loss in your adult life. It leads to a belief that if you really like something, it will probably be taken away from you, be it money, a career, a car, a nice pair of shoes, or anything you consider important. These are all the beliefs we need to un-program from our subconscious mind so that we're not making decisions as adults based on our childhood experiences.

Let's say you've been focused on identifying your life purpose and found a career fulfilling your soul, but you're barely surviving with the cash flow it's bringing you. More than likely, it's because you've heard or repeated phrases like this: Money doesn't grow on trees, or too much money causes problems in the family.

Or you compare yourself to others who are successful and think, "I'll never be able to make that." These are limiting beliefs about money which will prevent you from having the flow of income you desire even if you have found your life purpose and mission.

What are ways to reprogram the subconscious mind to eliminate these un-serving beliefs? We discussed sound therapy earlier, which can be great for reprogramming the mind. There are many meditation methods, some of which have been popularized more than others.

The Silva Ultramind method teaches you how to get to alpha and theta brain waves within seconds. Once you're in the theta wavelength, you can speak directly to your subconscious mind. This is where you would undo that negative money belief to say, "I am worthy of the wealth I desire. Health and wealth are a natural part of my being."

Your relationship with money, your career, health, or anything that you're struggling with at the moment can shift by reprogramming your subconscious mind. The best part is that you can learn it for free through books or online or use a coach or healer who can guide you to your specific needs.

The One Command method teaches you how to get to theta through a visualization process of connecting to the light above while being rooted to the earth and its magnetic and brilliant energy. The One Command starts with, "I don't know how. I'm in the best health ever. I only know it is so now, and I am fulfilled." This phrase prevents your conscious mind from creating resistance because you're telling yourself that you don't know how it's possible, which then puts your mind in agreement with you, so the next part of the statement is digestible and agreeable.

There are leaders in the industry, like Dr. Bruce Lipton and Dr. Joe Dispenza, and an entire platform of methods on MindValley.com, led by Vishen Lakhiani, which can support you on this journey. Find something that resonates with you and stay at it until you feel a shift in your external world. Living your best life requires working on yourself daily and doing the work to live in freedom.

NITA PATEL

About Nita Patel: Nita is a bestselling author, speaker, and artist who believes in modern etiquette as a path to becoming our best selves. Through her professional years, Ms. Patel has twenty-five years of demonstrated technology leadership experience in various industries specifically with a concentrated focus in health care for fourteen of those twenty-plus years. She's shown her art across the world including the Louvre in Paris.

She's a bestselling author and performance coach, pursuing her master's in industrial organizational (I-O) psychology at Harvard. Her investment in psychology theory and practice is what led her to a deep interest in helping others. She has become deeply and passionately devoted to nurturing others and in building their confidence and brand through speaking and consultative practices.

Author's Website: *www.Nita-Patel.com*

Book Series Website: *www.The13StepsToRiches.com*

Olga Geidane

THE LIES YOU TELL YOURSELF

What is subconscious?

Whilst you can't touch it, smell it, feel it, or hear it, your subconscious is mega powerful and carries 100% responsibility for what and how you do anything in life.

It is like a black box on the plane, with a big difference there: the black box is recording all data for the last 25 hours of the aircraft, whilst your subconscious does it from the time when you were in your mother's womb until right this moment.

Now, imagine that the black box started to work in a very strange way because, at some point, a faulty program was installed.

For example, one day, pilots, whilst being parked, were forced to stop the running engines because of a strong thunderstorm and had to wait until it had passed before starting the engines again and moving to the runway. This was done to keep everyone, including the aircraft itself, *safe*.

So, now just imagine for a second that the black box decided it is not safe by default every single time when there is rain or thunder. And it just automatically, by default, switches off the engines, thinking this is much safer—without analyzing the situation, like whether the plane is in the air or parked.

So that's exactly what your subconscious does. At some point in your life, especially when you were little, it learned on your behalf that a particular situation is not safe, is not making you feel good, is not beneficial for you, and therefore some actions must be taken to keep you safe and happy.

Whilst it was learning this, it also learned what your life is like while it recorded the movie around you 365 days a year, twenty-four hours a day. Your subconscious is constantly playing that for you in the background.

So, what is the connection between the black box and the movie? Actually, it's very straightforward: they are working alongside each other all the time!

Why do you end up in a relationship with someone just like your dad or like your mom when you were totally against the way they were when you experienced them as a child? Then, you wonder why you struggle to succeed even though you do all the right things just like everyone else, whilst you remember the lack of money in your own family when you were growing up.

Perhaps you are struggling to lose weight despite you doing everything—calorie counting, gym workouts, excessive exercising, watching what you eat and nearly starving yourself—without realizing that your programming is "to be a big girl" because you had to go out and provide for your family whilst your mom was an alcoholic…

Let me just put it this way, and you will not like it, but it is worth hearing it: You do not live your own life. Your subconscious lives your life on behalf of you. Your subconscious totally and completely controls your behavior, actions, choices, and beliefs based on multiple default programs. This means you are never truly free until the day you liberate yourself from default programs that don't serve you and install brand new ones.

Is that even possible?

Yes, it is. And it should be done as soon as possible. The best time for you was when you left your family and became independent, so you were not espoused to their programs anymore.

The second-best time is now.

Will you take charge of your subconscious or not? That is your choice. I am just here to open the door of possibilities for you. And, as Morpheus said in the movie *Matrix,* it's up to you to walk through that door.

So, how can you replace those default programs that, in many cases, don't serve us?

First, you've got to be completely honest and transparent with yourself: Are you truly, ultimately, 100% happy with your life, and every single aspect of your life? Is it the way you always wanted that to be? Are you proud of it?

If the answer is YES, I would invite you to sit quietly and truly connect with your heart and go deep there and ask yourself those questions again.

Why?

Because, very often, your subconscious is making you lie to yourself because it doesn't want to be called out and changed, as a result.

Just to give you an example, you might tell yourself that you are very happy being single, you really enjoy your life, and everything is fabulous as you date here and there, see anyone you want and whenever you want, change as many partners as you want and perhaps, even date multiple of them at the same time, because it's FUN.

It sounds like FUN, right? Freedom, liberation, adventures!

And perhaps, answering the question of whether you are happy that way, you will say: "Oh yes, at least I have my freedom and I don't have to deal with stupid arguments and routine in relationships!" Well, that is exactly how your subconscious lies to you: You are happy *because* you don't have to deal with stupid arguments and routines in relationships!

This actually means that you are stuck in a story that committed relationships equal, arguments, routine, loss of freedom. And the fear of that is keeping you away from attracting your soulmate.

And, on the question, "Is that the way you always wanted to be?" you would say: "No, but I will rather be single than be with some idiots; at least this way I rely only on myself and I don't depend on anyone providing for me."

This is how, again, your subconscious is telling you totally beautiful lies to make you believe that this is MUCH SAFER than probably it was when you were little. However, not being with anyone on a constant, long-term basis is bringing you more stress than you are even able to recognize. So, you are stuck in a vicious cycle of lying to yourself.

And then if I ask you, "Are you proud of the way your life is now?" you might say, "No, but it is easier this way…," which is another lie.

Your subconscious makes you believe it's easier this way because, most likely, what you have seen when you were growing up is a struggle and power fight in your family.

To help you with calling out the truth rather than listening to lies, I am inviting you to grab a pen and paper and answer the following questions again, but in writing and in fine detail, going through multiple areas of your life: Your relationships, money, health, well-being, career, spirituality, social circle, and more.

1. Are you truly, ultimately, 100% happy with the (pick one at the time: relationships, money, health, well-being, career, spirituality, social circle or other) aspect of your life?

2. Is it the way you always wanted that area to be?

3. Are you proud of how this area of your life is there now?

Take your time answering these questions. Don't rush. See what comes out.

What can you do with all that new information? Ideally, take it to your coach or a mentor and allow them to help you to replace all those fearful limiting beliefs with new, empowering stories that will help you to create your own future instead of living a default one.

Can you do it yourself? Sure, it just will take you longer and you might end up manipulated by your subconscious again. However, it is always worth trying!

Let me demonstrate to you how. Let's go back to our single person, who was actually…myself! It was me being stuck in all those lies that were sounding pretty fun for a while!

Remember the stories?

Committed relationships equal arguments, routine, and loss of freedom.

Is it true? Always ask yourself this question, as this way you are calling out the truth with the lie! The reality is: This is what I OBSERVED when I was growing up, so it wasn't my truth or my reality. It was something I grew up with and that became my "normal."

What is your new truth then? My new, chosen, individual truth is that I can be free and adventurous in my relationship with a partner that is able to discuss things and we always find ways how to talk more.

With that new story—there are no fears anymore. There is no need to run away from relationships anymore because from that moment onwards I would be not choosing someone matching my past story and old fears, but I will be attracting and choosing different profiles of people.

And just like that—with a few questions, you address and place under the flashlight the lies your subconscious says to you, and replace them with your new stories.

A little warning here: You will have MORE than one story, just like I had and all of my clients always have more than one story! The best part is:

By changing all of them, one by one, it will lead you to the next level of your life! And here is the cherry on top of the cake: It will be your own fabulous, amazing life that you have created!

And just as now I am happy and fulfilled in my real and authentic marriage, whilst traveling globally full time together with my husband, having plenty of adventures and passion, you will be able to create and design your own life based on your own new empowering stories!

OLGA GEIDANE

About Olga Geidane: Ready to outperform yourself? Meet Olga Geidane, the well-traveled keynote speaker, bestselling author, and award-winning mindset coach who's taking the world by storm! With her contagious energy and passion for personal growth, Olga has become a go-to expert for high achievers seeking to unleash their full potential. Whether you're an executive, entrepreneur, or simply someone who refuses to settle for mediocrity, Olga is here to guide you on your journey to success. But Olga's impact doesn't stop there.

As a firm believer in the power of love and connection, she organizes transformative couple retreats that breathe new life into partnerships, reigniting the flames of passion and understanding. Whether you're in the honeymoon phase or facing challenges, Olga's retreats are designed to help you build a stronger, more fulfilling relationship. And for those who have experienced the pain of infidelity, Olga's groundbreaking program offers a lifeline of support and healing.

Combining her expertise in mindset coaching and her own personal journey, she empowers victims of infidelity to overcome their trauma and rebuild their lives with strength and resilience. Ready to take your life to the next level? Join forces with Olga Geidane and unlock the extraordinary within you.

Author's Website: *www.OlgaGeidane.com*

Book Series Website: *www.The13StepsToRiches.com*

Phillip D. McClure

SUBCONSCIOUS BRAVERY

So, there I was. Yes, I'm starting it out like every other epic story you have ever heard. It was an early and dark morning as I was driving to work at 4:30 AM. Nothing was out of the ordinary; not many cars were out on the freeway at that hour. Then, all of a sudden, this beautifully restored old pickup truck comes driving past me—I remember because I was admiring the good-looking restoration job done on it. As I watched the truck get about 100 yards ahead of me, it looked as if it did not make the left turn on the freeway and flew right off the embankment. It simply just disappeared.

As I was getting closer, the truck came flying through the air as he had corrected and launched himself back onto the freeway. It was just like the Hollywood movies: Slow motion flying truck about twenty meters in front of me—mind you I was doing about 80 MPH when he passed me so there was some serious momentum happening. The pickup connected with the asphalt on its nose and erupted into flames. It then began flipping ass over tea kettle until it went sideways and was violently ripping itself apart as it rolled. It was all I could do to dodge all the wreckage being left and the parts flying past me.

Once the vehicle came to a standstill, completely flipped over on the top and engulfed by fire, I pulled my vehicle to the side of the road and began running towards the truck. The flames were so hot and I could see the man trapped and bucked in with arms hanging, completely unconscious. I then laid down on my back and started wiggling and sliding into the crushed window with all the broken glass and fluids leaking out of the wreckage. I was very grateful I was in my Army uniform at the time so it had some protection for me against the glass and heat.

It was horrific inside. The light from the flames showed blood dripping everywhere down on me, as his arm had been caught out of the window while rolling and the flesh was ground down pretty deep and he had a head would. I reached up and checked to see if he had a pulse, which he did. I then managed to get him unbuckled and did my best to help him fall safely, but it did not go as smoothly as planned. Then we both had to get out of the vehicle, which seemed to take forever. Adrenalin and the fire were helping me move quickly, though.

As I reached down to pick him up and carry him to my vehicle to give him first aid and get him away from the burning truck, another bystander stopped to help. I asked him to pick up his legs and I would carry his body and support his neck. As soon as we picked him up, he dropped him. So, we did it again and he dropped him again. This happened three times. I then laid the wounded man down and looked at the helper in the eyes and calmly told him to take three breaths (I WAS SCREAMING INSIDE MY MIND, THOUGH, AS THIS TRUCK COULD BLOW UP AT ANY SECOND!). He did, then I counted to three and told him to slowly pick him up and we then smoothly carried him to the front of my car where I could see him and assess him better.

Once I got him under the headlights of my vehicle, I was able to start patching him up and assessing the damages. I feel it inappropriate to go into detail beyond this point. Once the paramedics arrived, I was able to give them a report on the person and they took over and whisked him away in an ambulance. I then washed up in another ambulance, changed and had to throw away my uniform top and went to work like nothing happened.

However, I missed some blood on the back of one of my legs and then had some explaining to do. Turned out, another soldier was driving to work and saw the carnage and was talking about it before I got there. It was quite the experience. It showed me that first responders and military people can go into autopilot where the untrained struggle with the overload of stressors that are going on.

So, how does this all feed into the power of the subconscious mind?

The power of the subconscious mind is a fascinating topic that has been studied and explored by scientists, psychologists, and spiritual leaders for decades. The subconscious mind is the part of our mind that operates below the level of our conscious awareness, and it has been shown to have a profound influence on our thoughts, emotions, behaviors, and even our physical health.

One of the most incredible examples of the power of the subconscious mind can be seen in situations where someone's life is in danger and they are able to tap into a deep reservoir of inner strength and resilience to save themselves or others from harm. Let's explore the mechanics of the subconscious mind and how it works when dealing with a life-or-death situation such as a car crash.

The subconscious mind is responsible for much of our automatic behavior and responses to stimuli. It is constantly processing information from our environment and making split-second decisions about how to react to different situations. This is why we are able to walk, talk, and perform other complex tasks without consciously thinking about them. In a life-or-death situation such as a car crash, the subconscious mind can play a crucial role in determining whether or not someone survives.

When faced with a sudden and unexpected threat, the subconscious mind goes into overdrive, scanning the environment for potential dangers and activating the body's fight-or-flight response.

This response is a complex physiological process that involves the release of adrenaline and other stress hormones, which increase heart rate, blood pressure, and respiration. This surge of energy can provide a burst of strength and focus that can help someone escape from danger or save someone else's life.

In addition to the fight-or-flight response, the subconscious mind can also tap into deeper levels of awareness and intuition that are not accessible to the conscious mind. This is sometimes referred to as the "sixth sense" or "gut instinct," and it can provide valuable information and guidance in times of crisis.

Similarly, if someone else is trapped in the burning car, their subconscious mind may be able to tap into a deep reserve of strength and courage that enables them to take heroic action. They may feel a sudden surge of adrenaline and rush towards the car, putting their own safety at risk to rescue the trapped individual.

In the story above, the power of the subconscious mind was at work, providing guidance, strength, and resilience in the face of extreme danger and adversity. While we may not always be aware of the inner workings of our subconscious mind, it is clear that it plays a crucial role in our ability to survive and thrive in challenging situations.

We are in charge of how our subconscious minds operate. It is built by our beliefs, habits, and the decisions we make. By continuing to have the right thoughts to create the right actions which fortify stronger habits, you will bring your subconscious to a higher playing field and allow you to operate with more confidence and precision when needed. This is because you are reinforcing the neuro-pathways on how you are to act and perform.

As a conclusion to this chapter, I'd like to say final special thank you to John Assaraf. Thank you for being a part of this book. Your influence through your courses and books have placed me in arenas I never thought before possible. It is a pleasure to be co-writing this with you as this opportunity was the reason I knew I needed to be a part of this.

Thank you all.

PHILLIP D. MCCLURE

About Phillip D. McClure: Phillip is married to the love of his life, Maaike McClure, and is a very proud father of two exciting kids. He was raised in the great state of Montana before moving to Utah.

Phil lives life to the fullest. His accomplishments consist of completing a full Ironman, and deploying four times with the Army, earning multiple decorations along the way—including two Utah crosses! This makes him the only soldier in history to receive that medal twice.

Currently, Phil is the Owner of NorthStar Coins, Events by NorthStar, the co-owner of P.B. Fast Cars, and recruits pilots for the Army Aviation program. It was during his last deployment that he accidentally created his first Mastermind and it has forever changed his life as well as the others involved. He mentors and coaches in self-improvement and physical fitness.

Phil is an exotic car enthusiast who spends as much time behind the wheel as possible, whether it is carving through canyons, ripping around the racetrack, or coaching others to see their potential. Competitive driving is the best therapy in the world.

Live life to the fullest and have fun while doing it. You don't get a rewind in life so take mistakes as the lessons they are and improve, but don't make the same mistakes twice.

Live in flow, not with the flow.

Author's Website: *www.NorthStarCoins.com*

Book Series Website: *www.The13StepsToRiches.com*

Robyn Scott

TECHNIQUES FOR TRANSFORMATION AND GROWTH

"The subconscious mind is the intermediary, which translates one's prayers into terms which Infinite Intelligence can recognize, presents the message, and brings back the answer in the form of a definite plan or idea for procuring the object of the prayer."
~ **Napoleon Hill,** *Think and Grow Rich,* **1937**

We like to think of the subconscious mind as its own universe—a microcosm of past patterns and future dreams, regrets and nostalgia, Visions in limbo, and everything in between. Liv, who's on the Benshen Creative team (and the mystical Tomb Raider behind Psychic Landscape), spent her Master's program exploring the Jungian concept of the threshold between the conscious and subconscious mind. Here's what she has to say about her lifelong pursuit in unpacking the human psyche:

"A major aspect of working with Jungian theory includes the imaginative bridge-building between our subconscious and our physical world, so that we're able to articulate experiences and emotions that are otherwise difficult to comprehend.

"Carl Jung refers to our subconscious as 'the part of the psyche which retains and transmits the psychological inheritance of mankind.' In other words, everything we know, everything we experience, is an amalgamation of the senses, recorded and stored in our subconscious. We are vessels of these experiences, full of possibility and intention.

"Our subconscious can be accessed through dream analysis, active imagination, depth psychology and meditation. When we work with the subconscious, we reveal the source of our issue, rather than the symptoms associated with it that manifest in our conscious reality. Once identified, we have the potential to transform, resulting in healthier, more positive thoughts and behaviors."

All to say, the subconscious is a powerful portal. Governing 97% of our mind, the subconscious is the driving force behind our conscious behaviors. The conscious mind—3% of the puzzle—simply follows what it is directed to do by the subconscious, which stores all of our beliefs about ourselves and the world...many of which were developed by the age of seven years old and shaped by those around us.

And while it stores many of our "shadows," it isn't a part of the mind that we can afford to neglect for fear of opening the mental Pandora's box. According to Napoleon Hill, the subconscious mind acts as a critical link between our deepest desires and Infinite Intelligence (or God, or the universe, or higher source energy) to sync up and make shit happen.

Think about it: If 97% of our brain makes up the subconscious and is the driving force behind our 3% conscious mind, then in reality, it's a very powerful tool; we just have to get it on our side. It is the home of our thoughts before they actualize: "Thoughts are truly things, for the reason that every material thing begins in the form of thought-energy," Hill writes.

Luckily, there are powerful tools we can employ to navigate and thrive within this 3D inner world. In this book, we discuss how to bring awareness and change to our subconscious programming, in an effort to break up with the patterns and habits that take up real estate without our conscious permission. As we actively clear the subconscious landscape of the beliefs that don't benefit us, we make space for what we REALLY want, to draw ever closer to our dream reality. But first, we have to turn on the lights.

Take a moment to think about the times in our lives that something got us emotionally worked up versus a time where something of that same nature/texture didn't faze our friends in the slightest—OR vice versa. Have you ever stopped to wonder, why does this move me and not them? Or why does this send them into a spiral and I don't react the same?

Our reactions are built upon all of the experiences we've had up until this very moment, which get stored in the archive of our subconscious. Some of those reactions were learned by observing those around us during our childhood. Others are ones that we developed as a response to all the things life threw our way—both the good and the not-so-good. Over time, our mind becomes programmed, if you will, to react a certain way based on our past experiences rather than allowing us to act in the way we wish to.

Think of it like a computer: The computer arrives with certain programs and software, just like us. Over time, the software gets outdated, starts to glitch, and needs an upgrade, just like us. This is where meditation comes is.

Meditation works the same way as Apple does when it asks us, "Do we want to upgrade our software?" Our daily meditation practice is literally a software update of the mind.

Sometimes, the programs of our unconscious serve us, like when we have powerful stories around money or have no problem calling in unconditional love. But, more often than not, those programs leave us feeling less than inspired or empowered with ourselves and our lives.

The beauty is that we have the ability to change that, and in turn, change the very world we show up in, every single day. When we meditate, we clean out the proverbial "bugs" and "software glitches," i.e. old patterns and programs that we no longer wish to engage in and want to change.

Over time and with practice, we increase our ability to act when a situation confronts us rather than react to it. It's our impulsive reactions that often get us off track vs. allowing ourselves the time and space to figure out how we want to respond. Think of the times when we've been too quick to spin a story about something or react to a situation without taking a moment to think about how we really want to engage with it.

In those cases, it often takes more time and energy to do damage control, and that very same time and energy could have been channeled into something more productive. And, of course, some of our patterns can be very old and deep, which is why we're huge fans of therapy over here at *Benshen.co*.

We want to approach our subconscious with curiosity, love, and a whole lot of excitement over the idea that we do, in fact, have the ability to rewire our circuits so we can shine brighter than ever. When we bring in a proverbial flashlight and pan over the shadows in this multidimensional landscape, we can begin to foster self-sovereignty where there might not have been.

We can take an objective lens and ask ourselves if certain patterns of behavior even align with who we are now or where we're going... or if they simply keep showing up because that's just what happened once a few decades ago. Ultimately, with a daily meditation practice, we can begin to release what no longer serves us.

EXERCISE: In order to break up with unnecessary subconscious programming, it's important to be open to rewiring the circuits in our mind and change our impulse to jump from A to Z. "Dealing With Your Own Mind" is a meditation that is very simple to do and only takes six minutes long.

By inhaling long and deep through the left nostril and exhaling through the mouth, we can begin to calm the nervous system and the entire mind and body. Try it for forty days, either practicing first thing in the morning to set the tone for the day or at night right before bed for a deep, restorative sleep.

HOW TO DO IT:

1. Sit in any comfortable position where the spine can be straight (either in a meditative seat on a cushion, sitting in a chair, or propped up in bed).

2. With your right thumb, close off the right nostril to inhale long and deep through the left nostril.

3. Exhale through the mouth.

4. Continue for six minutes.

5. To end, inhale deep through both nostrils...and then exhale through the mouth.

It comes down to habit, truly! Make it a habit to pour goodness and light into your subconscious. We have it running anyway—why not control what we feed our subconscious minds!?

www.benshen.co/journal/subconscious-the-landscape-of-the-unconscious

ROBYN SCOTT

About Robyn Scott: Robyn Scott is a Habit Finder Coach and has worked closely with the president, Paul Blanchard, at the Og Mandino Group. She is also a certified Master Your Emotions Coach through Inscape World. Robyn Scott is commonly known in professional communities as the Queen of Connection and Princess of Play. She has been working hard for the past nine years to hone her skills as a mentor and coach.

Scott strives to teach people to annihilate judgments, embrace their own stories, and empower themselves to rediscover who they truly are. Scott is an international speaker and also teaches how to present yourself on stage.

Her first book, *Bringing People Together: Rediscovering the Lost Art of Face-to-Face Connecting, Collaborating, and Creating* was released in August 2019 and was a bestseller in seven categories.

Author's Website: *www.RobynKayeScott.com*

Book Series Website: *www.The13StepsToRiches.com*

Dr. Shannon Whittington

SUBCONSCIOUS ACTIONS

Unlike other parts of our mind, your subconscious does not have a sense of humor; it's as matter-of-fact as it gets. Your subconscious is the hidden key that determines your destiny, and despite its mysterious nature, you have the capacity to change your subconscious for the better. When you use simple hacks to alter the way your subconscious mind operates, your thoughts change, which means your behaviors often follow suit, altering the path of your life. With that in mind, here are a few nifty tricks to hack your subconscious and start making your dreams a reality.

Determine Your Goals

The first step in tricking your subconscious is having a clear idea of what you want. Whether your goal is to nab a promotion at work, to start your own business, or to buy a new house, etc., it's important to determine what your goals are. I find that it especially helps to physically write down my goals because there's something inherently different in the act of writing something down as opposed to typing it on a computer.

Another tip in writing out your goals that I cannot recommend enough is to write them in the present tense. Instead of "I want a new car," write down—and repeat daily (I recommend first thing in the morning and the last thing at night)—"I have a new car." Instead of "I want to start my own consultancy group," write and repeat, "I own my own consultancy group." This seemingly insignificant little hack will trick your subconscious into thinking your goals are reality, meaning you will start to think and behave in ways that move you closer to actually achieving your goals.

Visualize It

Whether or not you consider yourself a visual learner, I highly recommend creating visual reminders of your goals. One common tactic to accomplish this is creating a vision board. To do this, simply go online and find images that represent your goals, print and crop them, and attach them to a poster board. You could also rummage through physical magazines and cut out clippings for your board. Be sure to hang the poster board in a location you know you'll be in every day.

If you want a new house, find an image of a house that speaks directly to you. If you want the perks of a new promotion, find images of your favorite car or an office space with a gorgeous view. If the idea of creating a physical vision board feels too cumbersome to you, you can simply create a Pinterest board or copy and paste images into a Google doc and look at it every morning and right before you go to sleep every night. You can even make it your screensaver! This will affect your subconscious by training your mind to work harder and dedicate yourself even more to achieving the things you want, and the more you view and absorb your vision, the closer you will find yourself to getting the things you want.

Determine (& Stop) Your Blockers

We all have blockers, a.k.a. things that prevent us from getting things done. Whether it's procrastination, fear of failure, a hectic work-life imbalance, etc., your blockers are what keep your subconscious mind in a state of arrested development. It's up to you to do everything you can to address these blockers and bring yourself closer to achieving your goals.

For example, if you're a procrastinator, hold yourself accountable to getting your daily tasks done by a certain time each day (or, ask one of your friends/colleagues to be your accountability partner to better ensure you're completing your tasks). If you find yourself constantly worried about failure, read articles or watch YouTube videos created by others who have had similar fears and have found ways to overcome them.

If you find that you have way too much going on throughout the day, consider sitting down and scheduling out your days so that you leave room for quiet time, meditation, or something else entirely so that you don't get too overwhelmed. Your blockers do not have to determine how you spend the rest of your life; they can be overcome and you will feel a tremendous sense of accomplishment when you address them.

Forgive Your Past Mistakes

For many of us, overcoming our mistakes and regrets can feel next to impossible. We're often our own biggest critics and we can often have a strong inclination to dwell on our mistakes, which makes achieving our goals even more difficult. Therefore, it's important to sit with yourself and actively forgive yourself for your past errors. Remember, you did what you knew how to do at the time! Dwelling on your mistakes won't change your past, but dwelling on them can definitely alter your future for the worse, which is why you owe it to yourself to move past your mistakes and make room for your wins.

Instead of thinking that you don't deserve to achieve your goals because of the mistakes you've made, congratulate yourself for having a learning experience and knowing what to do—or what not to do—moving forward. Whenever you have the compulsion to think about a mistake or regret, immediately shift your focus to a time in your life that you're proud of. Each time you do this, your subconscious will move from a mentality of "I'm a screw-up" to "I am a person who deserves the best."

Embrace the Right Media

Ask yourself: "How am I spending my down time?" Are you spending most of your free time vegging out and watching Netflix or scrolling? If so, there's a ton of unused potential that you're not opening yourself to. (Just view your media screen time summary and you might see what I mean.) Your subconscious is fueled by the things you do and the content you consume every day, which is why you owe it to yourself to watch, read, and listen to the right media.

Instead of spending all your free time watching your favorite shows, set a limit for yourself and spend your free time reading books and listening to podcasts/watching YouTube videos related to your goals. If you can't make this an everyday habit, try your best to aim for every other day. The more of this type of content you consume, the more hardwired your subconscious will become to pursuing your goals.

Ignore (or Celebrate) the Haters

No matter who are, what you do, or what you believe, there are always going to be individuals who dislike you, look down on you, or do not approve of what you do. You could run the world's largest nonprofit and do unspeakably great work every day, and I can guarantee that there will be those who despise you for what you do; it's simply a fact of life. Further, said hatred has the power to affect your subconscious mind if you let it, which is why, instead of letting others' negativity get to your head or harboring resentment toward them, simply ignore them.

Understand that your haters are on their own path and have chosen to spend their time focusing on you, and it's up to you to ignore their hate. Or, if you have the time to spare to acknowledge it, treat their criticism as a good thing! If someone has dedicated their precious free time to disparage you for the path you're on, you're clearly doing something worthy of attention. You can also use this as an opportunity to surround yourself with others who get you and understand the incredible things you're doing, giving your subconscious something positive to embrace in place of others' negativity.

Keeping all of these tactics in mind is not always easy; in fact, it may take weeks, if not longer, of rewiring your subconscious to make these actions into habits. But I promise you that the more you commit to these actions, the more your mind will alter and the more your actions will follow suit. You owe it to yourself to trick your subconscious, and your subconscious will thank you for it in the long-term.

SHANNON WHITTINGTON

About Dr. Shannon Whittington: Shannon (she/her) is a speaker, author, consultant, and clinical nurse educator. Her area of expertise is LGBTQ+ inclusion in the workplace. Whittington has a passion for transgender health where she educates clinicians in how to care for transgender individuals after undergoing gender-affirming surgeries.

Whittington was honored to receive the Quality and Innovation Award from the Home Care Association of New York for her work with the transgender population. She was recently awarded the Notable LGBTQ+ Leaders & Executives award by Crain's New York Business, Daisy Award for Outstanding Nurses, as well as the International Association of Professionals Nurse of the Year award. Whittington is a city and state lobbyist for transgender equality.

To date, Whittington has presented virtually and in person at various organizations and conferences across the nation, delivering extremely well-received presentations. Her forthcoming books include *LGBTQ+: ABC's For Grownups* and *Kindergarten for Leaders: 9 Essential Tips For Grownup Success.*

Author's Website: *www.linkedin.com/in/ShannonWhittington*

Book Series Website: *www.The13StepsToRiches.com*

Soraiya Vasanji

HEALING YOUR SUBCONSCIOUS

You are powerful.

Your brain is powerful.

Yet, we are not even aware that the majority of our thoughts inform our actions. Your brain's neural network controls the thoughts, beliefs, actions and how you show up every day of your life. In general, the mind operates on three levels: the conscious, the subconscious and the unconscious. Did you know that 95% of our brain activity is unconscious? Scientists estimate that 50-60% of this activity can be attributed to the subconscious. Conversely, we are only fully aware and making conscious choices from 5% of our brain. This is why the subconscious mind is extremely powerful and it's important to learn how to harness and access its power to create your best abundant life.

Generally, our *consciousness* is defined as our thoughts, actions, and awareness; consciousness is grounded in the present moment and is usually hyper aware of one task at a time. For example, in this moment I am reading; in this moment I am breathing; in this moment I am thinking about whether I am reading or breathing. The *subconscious mind* works underneath the conscious level and drives our actions and behaviors from stored beliefs, thoughts, and memories.

One clear example is when you were learning to drive a car: turning the steering wheel and shifting gears was in your consciousness. Many years later, we find ourselves getting into our car and not being aware of the drive over but arriving at our destination—this was our subconscious at play. The *unconscious mind* is the deeply stored memories, and generational downloads of our past. Do you remember what it felt like when you first learned to walk? Most of us can't recall that moment and this is an example of what is in our unconscious mind.

Our subconscious mind is constantly working and is generally on autopilot. When you stop to think about it, the little actions that you are doing right now go unnoticed by your awareness—how you turned the page, or washed the dishes, or folded the laundry. When you first learn a new skill, you are aware and present to the intricacies but after you have been doing it awhile and developed the skill your mind goes elsewhere, and the task still gets complete. An example of this is when I first learned to knit. I would need to count each stitch so that I didn't miss a stitch. Nowadays, I can be watching Netflix and my fingers are rhythmically working through the pattern without looking down.

The subconscious holds our beliefs and thoughts that influence our actions without us being aware of these notions. This is the critical part: Not being fully aware of the thoughts we are using as the foundation of our choices. In a way, our subconscious has the blueprint that keeps us comfortable and safe. Think of your subconscious like a set point on a thermometer. Your beliefs keep you in a narrow pendulum. For example, if your subconscious is set to 72 degrees, then all the choices we make in the present bring us near those 72 degrees. If we set a new goal which would land us near 90 degrees, we will still aim for it but land south of 90 degrees and typically closer to 72 degrees. We are creatures of habit and don't like to be outside our comfort zone if we don't have to.

That is why it takes time to form a new habit because a complex neural network needs to be rewired and to move our subconscious set point takes time. Every January, millions of people choose a New Year's resolution to hit the gym and lose weight. By the end of January, 90% of them have quit and by the end of February another 9% of people quit their weight loss resolution. That 1% is different because they choose to create new rules and shift their paradigm thinking. In order to set ourselves up to succeed, we must tap into the subconscious mind and reframe that 72 degrees closer to 90 degrees. We must shift our thinking and see ourselves as gym bunnies and not couch potatoes.

We are constantly self-regulating and bringing ourselves back to our comfort zone. Sometimes, however, our subconscious can derail our goals and sabotage us because we hold toxic or disempowering beliefs about ourselves. I call it the subconscious saboteur. It is our inner critic voice who holds us back with that negative self-talk. I have come to believe that beyond our own self-talk voice, we carry the generational load of knowledge and trauma from generations before us.

It is beautiful to honor the wisdom in our makeup but it's time we work through that trauma so it ends with us and we don't pass along those beliefs to the next generation. Let's be the generation that breaks those chains and leaves an elevated pathway for our legacy. We get to have generational healing and the rebuilding of our power lines and strength.

One example of a deeply rooted belief in my people, who are refugees from East Africa and came to Canada with just a suitcase and an ethos for hard work, is the idea that we should not spend money on gifts, parties, or elaborate celebrations for milestones like birthdays or anniversaries. It is better to save this money and keep it for food, shelter, education, or an emergency. This deeply rooted belief, at its core, was a solid framework to support thousands of families to climb the social and economic ladder and provide for their families.

Decades ago, this belief was needed to live with a mindset of getting the basic necessities and surviving day-to-day, and then as they elevated their status this belief reinforced their desire to save money and send their children to university. Fast forward to the present, and it's these deeply rooted beliefs that hold us back on celebrating ourselves, hold us back from receiving love from others in the form of celebrating us, and hold us back from opening our hearts and receiving without judgment or expectation.

Showering your love and kindness on someone is an act of giving. But it also takes an open heart and mind to receive this love and acknowledge it. The cycle of giving and receiving needs to be equal in the universe. If you just give and don't receive, you are being selfish in not opening yourself up to someone giving their love to you. Likewise, if you are a taker and you receive but don't give, you will never know the deepest, purest love of what it is to give unconditionally to someone.

My grandparents' generation does not want lavish celebrations for their birthday. However, when they are in the presence of all those who love them, their elevated pride, joy, and love is palpable. On the outside, they are physically shaking their head as it is hard for them to acknowledge the time, energy, money, and showering of love in this way—not because they don't want to, but because their subconscious overrides their moment of joy and before they know it, their words are dismissing all of these kind gestures as a waste of money and time.

It is time to shift our subconscious narrative and rewire how we give and receive love. Let it be independent of money and instead weighted in the value of feeling seen, heard, and loved. Tapping into the subconscious and working to shift our beliefs and thoughts is important to creating the abundant and joy-filled life we are meant to have. It starts with our mindset.

In my signature Mom Mindset Reset Method Coaching Program, we always start with tuning and observing our mindset from a place of neutrality. It has been estimated that 96% of our thoughts are negative. They are negative because we are constantly replaying the past and reviewing our history for what we did wrong and what we should do differently next time.

Instead, get super present. Observe your current thoughts without judgment, in a place of neutrality. What are you doing and feeling right now? Utilize the power of all of your senses to get present. What do you touch? Taste? Hear? Smell? See? We start to rewire the neural connections in the brain when we start forcing ourselves out of old habits and into new ones. That's why affirmations and speaking positively to yourself are crucial.

The subconscious mind does not differentiate between positive or negative, so if you say you can't do something, then your mind believes it; but if you say you can do something, then your mind believes that. Whether or not it is true is independent of the cataloging of the mind. If you consistently speak positive messages to yourself, your new normal will be a positive outlook. Over time, you will come to see yourself and your world differently. Once your way of being has shifted everything in your life will shift to the positive.

Beyond harnessing the power of positivity, embrace gratitude. It may seem strange or like you are already doing this, but living life through the lens of gratitude is freeing and paints everything around us in abundance. Start by identifying ten things that you are grateful for. I used to say three things but over time I found the clients who were writing down ten or more things they were grateful for were having much better results. They were manifesting a greater abundance because their subconscious was on the scavenger hunt for how they felt grateful even when they were not present to it.

Cultivate your sense of gratitude, use the power of positive language, and observe your thoughts so you can heal the underlying beliefs and you will be on your path to abundance both consciously and subconsciously.

SORAIYA VASANJI

About Soraiya Vasanji: Soraiya is a Certified Professional Coach (CPC), Energy Leadership Index Master Practitioner (ELI-MP), and has a Master's in Business Administration (MBA) from Kellogg University. She inspires women to be present, not perfect, ditch what doesn't serve them, and create their best messy life now.

She loves sharing her wisdom on mindset, the power of language, self-love, self-worth, and leadership principles. She is the founder of the Mommy Mindset Summit series, and the Mom Mindset Reset Method coaching program. She empowers moms to move from tired, frustrated and depleted in their life to a creating the calm, happy and emotional even life for them and their families - no longer swinging from "energizer bunny mom" to dead on the couch!

Soraiya is married to her soulmate, has a young daughter, and lives in Toronto, Canada. She is a foodie, a jetsetter, a doTERRA essential oil enthusiast, and she loves collecting unique crafting and stationery products!

Author's Website: *www.SoraiyaVasanji.com*

Book Series Website: *www.The13StepsToRiches.com*

Stacey Ross Cohen

TAP INTO THE POWER OF THE SUBCONSCIOUS MIND

"The reason man may become the master of his own destiny is because he has the power to influence his own subconscious mind."
~ **Napoleon Hill**

The Subconscious Mind Defined

Often referred to as the "inner voice," the subconscious mind is essentially a powerful data processor. It captures inputs—like thoughts and environmental stimuli—from all areas of our lives, and then synthesizes them into our behaviors, emotions, and decisions. Our subconscious mind never rests, either: In addition to synthesizing, it's always on call controlling our heartbeat, digestion, and other vital body functions. And it's also communicating with our conscious mind, influencing how we think and feel.

Here's the great news: You are essentially the "programmer" of your subconscious mind. With a little practice, you can carve any idea, purpose, plan, or goal into it to help achieve unparalleled levels of personal and professional growth. In essence, you are the boss!

In this chapter, we will focus on some tools and techniques to harness your subconscious mind. Remember, we choose what we feed our subconscious minds—for better or worse.

Positivity Rules

"Where focus goes, energy flows," Tony Robbins famously says. This adage is especially relevant when it comes to the subconscious. It means: You are the creator of your thoughts. It's your call what you want to direct your attention to. So, choose wisely—because what you focus on expands and intensifies.

Those who focus on the bad tend to experience more of it. We all know a "Debbie Downer" who always has new health issues or can't hold down a job. These people often blame external circumstances when the real problem lies within.

But the sky becomes the limit when we shift our focus to positive goals and actions. When you choose to think positively, also choose to be kind to yourself. Banish self-limiting thoughts and practice self-compassion. It allows you to enter a "flow state," where one positive thought leads to another.

Once you make the conscious choice to think positively, make a routine. And be thorough about it—a promise is one thing, but a regimen is another. Let this be your inspiration: About five years ago, I visited a K-8 independent private school nestled in the Sonoma, California wine region for a story I was writing for HuffPost. The school abounds with inquisitive students, supportive families, and progressive faculty and staff.

Their secret? A commitment to positive thinking at an early age. Each day begins with mindfulness practice: Two minutes for kindergarten students, building up to twenty minutes by the time students are in fifth grade. UC Berkeley's Greater Good Science Center defines mindfulness as "a moment-by-moment awareness of our thoughts, feelings, bodily sensations, and surrounding environment." Research indicates that mindfulness yields better concentration, reduced anxiety, and heightened social skills.

So, as you're being mindful, which emotions should you pursue? According to Hill, there are seven primary positive emotions: desire, faith, love, sex, enthusiasm, romance, and hope. And there are seven major negative emotions: fear, jealousy, hatred, revenge, greed, superstition, and anger. Positive and negative emotions cannot exist simultaneously; only one can dominate. By disciplining your mind to only allow positive emotions to prevail, you prevent negative emotions from entering.

This kind of positivity is a vital tool. And for me, it's personal. At age forty-eight, my mom became severely ill while vacationing with friends. A local doctor dismissed her symptoms as a mere stomach virus and prescribed a soak in the bathtub. But after thirty-six hours, there was no improvement. My father took my mom to the nearest hospital by ferry and learned the actual diagnosis was severe: She had suffered a massive heart attack, had lost 70% function of her heart, and had just three months to live.

But my mom ended up living until age sixty-five. Why? Because of her positivity. She spent the next seventeen years wearing heart monitors and visiting emergency rooms, but always believed she would be okay. She was incredibly positive, and I rarely heard her complain.

In fact, she lived selflessly, from inviting "strays" to Thanksgiving, to covering her hospital roommate's television fees, to countless other kindnesses. My mom's positivity and faith granted her an extra seventeen years with her family—and also taught us the importance of positivity.

Fueling the Subconscious Mind

As Thomas Edison aptly said, "Choose your thoughts carefully." Just as we feed our bodies, we must also feed our minds "healthy" thoughts. How? You can harness the power of your subconscious mind by following these five best practices:

- **Banish Self-Limiting Beliefs & Negative Self-Talk:** As mentioned above, positive and negative thoughts can't coexist. It's your responsibility to ensure positive emotions dominate your mind.

- **Boost Your Desire:** Your subconscious mind acts on thoughts conveyed with desire. When your goal becomes a consuming obsession, and you have a burning desire to realize it, success is around the corner.

- **Establish Goals:** Make sure to write down your goals. Then, reinforce them: Read your goal aloud after waking up and before going to sleep, and visualize yourself already in possession of your desire. Once you clearly define and prioritize your goals, you will be better positioned to make decisions to achieve them.

- **Persistence/Consistent Repetition:** Develop the habit of applying and using positive emotions. The most critical times of day to practice this habit are upon waking and before you hit the pillow. *Don't* reach for your cell phone when you wake up. Instead, set the tone for the day by taking a few minutes to practice gratitude or meditation. And before sleep, consider goals you'd like to accomplish tomorrow, or mull over questions to which you are seeking a solution.

- **Embrace Positive Affirmations:** Affirmations are simple phrases you repeat regularly to internalize and emphasize thoughts, like "I am strong." These affirmations should be stated in the present tense as if the result has already occurred. I use affirmations to ace new business opportunities, grow my agency, and empower my team. If you're seeking an affirmation but need inspiration, consider one of these:

  - I am a success in all that I do.

  - I'm open to new adventures in my life.

  - My business is growing and thriving.

  - My needs and wants are important.

  - I'm worthy of love.

  - I am conquering/defeating my illness.

  - I act with courage and confidence.

The Importance of Visualization

A picture is worth a thousand words—and that holds true when it comes to harnessing your subconscious, too. When pursuing positivity, images tend to be more potent than words. Napoleon Hill said it best: "If you do not see great riches in your imagination, you will never see them in your bank balance."

Learn how to use visualization, the practice of creating vivid and desirable images in your mind. Indeed, "Seeing is believing" and "Visualize to materialize" are more than just motivational phrases—they are proven and effective psychological methods backed by science. Just ask the Olympians and professional athletes who use visualization to focus on and achieve victory.

To get started, create a detailed vision board with pictures, words, and quotes. You can also blend visualization with affirmation by writing your affirmations on Post-It notes. Another idea: printed "affirmation cards" that you can keep in your wallet. My close business colleague uses these.

Once, when I felt defeated about a new business pitch, he handed me a card that read, "I am successful at whatever I put my mind to." Set aside a few minutes a day to close your eyes and imagine your life *after* your goal has been achieved.

Meditate, Meditate, Meditate

I am a big proponent of meditation to clear your mind and spark creativity. An alert mind is better able to learn new things and create new ideas. There are various meditation methods that you can do to help increase your imagination. Look for ways to incorporate meditation techniques into your daily life—even if it's just for ten minutes a day. If you're seeking a helping hand, try using apps like Calm and Headspace.

Gratitude Matters

On your journey to harness your subconscious, gratitude will play a major role. Offer expressions of gratitude for what you have received in life, but also what you *hope* to receive. You reap what you plant in your subconscious mind. You can teach yourself that you are healthy, happy, good-looking, or mentally strong.

Your mind works like a magnet, drawing like things to you. So, send out positive thoughts, and your subconscious will attract rather than repel positivity to you—riches, prosperity, health, and all the good things in life. Remember, your thoughts are the blueprint of life, and when you channel your thinking, you create the conditions that make achieving your goals inevitable.

STACEY ROSS COHEN

About Stacey Ross Cohen: In the world of branding, few experts possess the savvy and instinct of Stacey. An award-winning brand professional who earned her stripes on Madison Avenue and major television networks before launching her own agency, Stacey specializes in cultivating and amplifying brands.

Stacey is CEO of Co-Communications, a marketing agency headquartered in New York. She coaches businesses and individuals across a range of industries—from real estate to healthcare and education—and expertly positions their narratives in fiercely competitive markets.

A TEDx speaker, Stacey is a sought-after keynote at industry conferences and author in the realm of branding, PR, and marketing. She is a contributor at Huffington Post and Thrive Global and has been featured in *Forbes, Entrepreneur, Crain's,* and a suite of other media outlets. She holds a B.S. from Syracuse University, an MBA from Fordham University, and a certificate in Media, Technology, and Entertainment from NYU Stern School of Business.

Author's Website: *www.StaceyRossCohen.com*

Book Series Website: *www.The13StepsToRiches.com*

Teresa Cundiff

A MOTHER-IN-LAW'S WISDOM

When I first pondered the topic of the subconscious mind, I thought I would read up on it and see what Freud had to say about it. It was fascinating reading for sure. I didn't realize that that are so many different explanations for what it is and what it does. It seems to lend itself to an analogy of the cell phone with open apps running in the background. However, those apps don't influence what the other apps are doing or what the user of the phone is viewing at any one time. So, that wasn't an accurate analogy at all, but it's the closest parallel I can draw.

Napoleon Hill says, "The subconscious mind consists of a field of consciousness in which every impulse of thought that reaches the objective mind through any of the five senses is classified and recorded, and from which thoughts may be recalled or withdrawn as letters may be taken from a filing cabinet." I love this explanation. I also love the way Hill writes. If you are reading this series of thirteen books but have yet to read *Think and Grow Rich* itself, you are robbing yourself of magic! I will go so far to say that reading Hill's chapter on our current subject and then reading this compilation book would serve you the best.

I will share a story with you from my own life about how my subconscious mind was governing a behavior I had, but I didn't realize it until it was pointed out to me by my mother-in-law, Mary Lou, who was a nurse working in mental health.

In August of 1975, when I was twelve years old, our home burned to the ground. It was built in the early 1900s and had three fireplaces. When we turned the corner up the driveway, the only things left standing were those three chimneys. The house was smoldering rubble with smoke still rising from it. We were left with only the clothes on our backs. It was devastating, to say the least.

My mom was in Orlando, Florida, attending my brother's graduation from Navy boot camp. My older sister, Lesa, fifteen at the time, and my younger sister, Tina, six at the time, and I were all in school as it had started the week before. My dad had taken off work for the day to take one of our TVs to the repair shop. I was called out of my classroom after lunch to go to the office. When I got there, they were inquiring as to the whereabouts of my dad. They were trying to contact him and couldn't locate him. I thought this was really strange, but being taught to respect authority and not question, I told them where I thought he was. I went back to class.

Within the same class period, I was again called to the office. Now, this happened over the room speaker where the office could talk to each classroom individually, so the whole class knew I was going to the office again. The speaker said, "Mrs. So-and-So, will you send Teresa Landers to the office?" There weren't really any oohs and aahs like I was in trouble since no one really knew anyone yet, but I was embarrassed, nonetheless. This trip to the office resulted in me getting information that someone from my church would be picking me up. Weird, but okay!

When the church friend arrived to pick me up, she already had my sister Lesa in the car with her. From my school, we went to the elementary school to pick up Tina. Being the naïve twelve-year-old that I was, I wasn't suspicious that something "bad" had happened, I just followed the directions given to me by the adults in my life. After collecting Tina, we went to Mrs. Morgan's house. She gave us snacks and said our dad would be there to pick us up.

The plan changed, and we piled In Mrs. Morgan's car and started for home. We lived out in the country on some property, so it wasn't a subdivision situation. When we made the turn on our road, she stopped the car and tearfully turned around and said, "It's all gone. You ain't got a house no more." Of course, my mind was reeling with this information because she didn't say it had burned down, she just said it was gone.

Right then, our dad pulled up, and we got out to see him. The look on his face was stoic. I still did not have a grip on what was happening. He said, "The house has burned down." I honestly can't remember if he said anything else after that, but we did have a group hug.

We got in the back of Dad's truck and rode slowly down the lane to what was left of our house. We arrived at the driveway, and he turned in and we all cast our eyes upon the smoldering ashes of what had been our home and the three chimneys standing there. It was a sight that is ingrained in my conscious, so it must be further ingrained in my subconscious. As I think back on it, my mind plays it in slow motion. We got out of the truck to walk closer to see better. The foundation of the house was held up by huge trees laid parallel across the foundation. This alone was a sight to see. These trees were what was still smoldering.

The story goes that by the time the fire department made it all the way out there; the fire was too engaged in doing anything other than manage it while it burned itself out. The fire department was not there when we arrived, as we learned that the fire started in the morning and by now it was late afternoon. The animals, Ladd, the collie dog, and Patches, the cat, had survived. Ladd was an outdoor dog, and we always put Patches out when we left for the day. My dad would say, "C.A.T. O.U.T," each morning when it was time, but she learned what those six letters meant and would go scrambling. It was always an adventure trying to get the cat out the door with us! Thank God we did!

I came to learn that the reason I had been called out of my class that day and asked about my dad's whereabouts was because the authorities were trying to locate all of us. There was a fear when they were talking to me that my dad had been lost in the fire! Think about that with me. The office staff at my school knew that my house had burned down and that my father was missing when they talked to me. That must have been agonizing for them to look at me and know that information. I have given the whole scenario much thought over all these years.

There's more to the story, of course, but I will leave it there. Here's what I can share that happened in my subconscious mind. Houses made of wood and aluminum siding, etc., can burn down. I'm going to have a house made of stone that will not burn down. Every time I would see a stone house, I would say, "I'm going to have a home like that when I get big."

I also have an awareness now, thanks to my mother-in-law noticing it, that I was always taking so many pictures. I always had my camera out and at the ready to capture all the precious moments. I did this because I didn't have any photos of my own childhood anymore. My mom had sent school photos to her parents which we got back, but everything was consumed in the fire—EVERYTHING! No toothbrush, no nightgown when nightfall was just a few hours away, no underwear to put on in the morning...nothing!

With my mom being out of town, I took advantage and wore my favorite jeans to school, which were kind of ratty (even though they are right in style now!), and my favorite pink tank top. Those, along with my socks, shoes, and underwear, were all I had to wear.

I know now and understand the subconscious things that happened to me then and still inform my decisions today, but I never made the correlation between my desire to capture my family's memories on film until Mary Lou made the connection. Once she did, I could look back on so many other things that losing my home at such a young age programmed me for in my subconscious. Taking to heart what Napoleon hill has to say about the "filing away" of memories into a cabinet puts a fine point on being consciously aware of what we allow to enter our minds.

Thoughts accompanied by feelings are what stick with us, so be very careful about what you experience because it will have a lasting impression. I had no control over my home burning down, of course, but I guard my heart and mind now and encourage you to do the same!

TERESA CUNDIFF

About Teresa Cundiff: Teresa hosts an interview digital TV show called Teresa Talks on Legrity TV. On the show, she interviews authors who are published and unpublished—and that just means those authors haven't put their books on paper yet. The show provides a platform for authors to have a global reach with their message. Teresa Talks is produced by Wordy Nerds Media Inc., of which Cundiff is the CEO.

Cundiff is also a freelance proofreader with the tagline, "I know where the commas go!" Teresa makes her clients work shine with her knowledge of grammar, punctuation, and sentence structure.

Teresa is a four-time international bestselling contributing author of 1 Habit for Entrepreneurial Success, 1 Habit to Thrive in a Post-COVID World, The Art of Connection: 365 Days of Networking Quotes and The Art of Connection: 365 Days of Inspirational Quotes. The latter two are both placed in the Library of Congress. She is a ten-time bestselling contributing author to *The 13 Steps to Riches* Series.

Author's Website: *www.TeresaTalksTv.com*

Book Series Website: *www.The13StepsToRiches.com*

Vera Thomas

TRANSFORMATION

Transformed
by the renewing of our mind
It is just a matter of time
Those thoughts become things
The subconscious mind brings
Into reality
Those thoughts our mind believes
Retrieve positivity to replace doubt
Retrieve your faith watch fear fade out
Retrieve love and hate will not abide
Let imagination, desire and faith be your guide
The manifestation of your subconscious
Is how success will thrive.

In Napoleon Hill's chapter on the topic of the subconscious mind, I noticed how he relates faith and prayer as integral in achieving the manifestation of what the mind can conceive. In fact, Hill says, "Prayer does, sometimes, result in the realization of that which one prays. If you have ever had the experience of receiving that for which you prayed, go back in your memory, and recall your actual STATE OF MIND while you were praying, and you will know for sure, that the theory here described is more than a theory." He also said, "Faith is the only known agency which will give your thoughts a spiritual nature."

He also refers to desire, imagination, auto suggestion and transmutation as components to developing your subconscious into a positive force.

With all this in mind, I want to reflect on faith and prayer and the subconscious mind. Keep in mind that our subconscious is active 24/7 and absorbs everything, positive or negative. We can control what we allow to dominate our subconscious mind, which is manifested into our reality.

There are over 100 scriptures referring to our subconscious. I would like to expound on a few.

Romans 12:2: *Do not be conformed to this world, but be transformed by the renewal of your mind, that by testing, you may discern what is the will of God, what is good, acceptable, and perfect.*

Renewing our mind requires awareness. Hill states, "Transformation can be given only through your own subconscious mind." Renewing our minds requires being still through meditation, focusing on things spiritual and universal, and allowing our minds to take us beyond what we see, beyond what we are experiencing, and beyond what appears to be.

Through meditation, we are going beyond what appears to be reality and focusing in on what the spirit or universe deems for us. It allows us to let go and let the spirit or the universe take control. Imagination kicks in to allow for the realization of desire. Thoughts become things that are transforming.

Philippians 4:8 ESV: *Finally, brothers, whatever is true, whatever is honorable, whatever is just, whatever is pure, whatever is lovely, whatever is commendable, if there is any excellence, if there is anything worthy of praise, think about these things.*

This is one of my favorite scriptures. Getting these thoughts into our self-conscious will result in less stress and more sense of contentment in whatever state we may find ourselves. Accentuate the positives and the negatives will soon subside. It is about your mindset! During meditation, think on these things. Throughout the course of your day, think on these things.

Hill states, "Positive and negative emotions cannot occupy the mind at the same time." With daily practice, positive thoughts will soon become innate in your subconscious. You will find yourself not wanting to be around negative people.

Colossians 3:2 ESV: *Set your minds on things that are above, not on things that are on earth.*

This scripture is very consistent with the concepts of transmutation. When we elevate our thoughts, we elevate our life.

1 Peter 4:7 ESV: *The end of all things is at hand; therefore, be self-controlled and sober minded for the sake of your prayers.*

I once had a sign on my refrigerator that said, "Why pray if you are going to worry? Why worry if you pray?" Hill says, "...no one will approach the Universal Mind in a state of fear..." Your subconscious mind will receive what you give.

Philippians 4:6-7 ESV: *Do not be anxious about anything, but in everything by prayer and supplication with thanksgiving let your requests be made known to God. And the peace of God, which surpasses all understanding, will guard your hearts and your minds in Christ Jesus.*

For those who believe in the Universe or some other faith, this applies as well. Allow your subconscious mind to concentrate on the spirit of thanksgiving. If we focus on what we are thankful for, I believe our subconscious mind will allow us to attract more positivity than negativity. There is nothing like peace of mind. When we are anxious, fearful, or doubtful, those things disturb our peace. You cannot experience peace when your mind is filled with negative thoughts.

Psalm 19:14 ESV: *Let the words of my mouth and the meditation of my heart be acceptable in your sight, O Lord, my rock and my redeemer.*

Before we utter a word, it is our first thought. Remember, we are what we think about all day long. Think about the thoughts you focus on the most throughout the day. Are they positive or negative? Do they uplift or tear down you and others?

Psalm 139:23-24 ESV: *Search me, O God, and know my heart! Try me and know my thoughts! And see if there is any grievous way in me and lead me in the way everlasting!*

The heart contains the thoughts that are within our mind. Our subconscious mind controls the heart—think about that.

Philippians 2:13 ESV: *For it is God who works in you, both to will and to work for his good pleasure.*

When the focus of our subconscious mind is positive the results will be the same.

Romans 7:25 ESV: *Thanks be to God through Jesus Christ our Lord! So then, I myself serve the law of God with my mind, but with my flesh I serve the law of sin.*

While I am writing from a Christian perspective, please know this applies to whatever your faith or belief. What matters is whether our subconscious mind is congruent with our faith.

Proverbs 18:8 ESV: *The words of a whisperer are like delicious morsels; they go down into the inner parts of the body.*

What are we subconsciously thinking? What are we saying to ourselves that will allow our subconscious mind to bring forth the good that is intended for us? Our subconscious mind clearly defines our existence.

Joshua 1:8 ESV: *This Book of the Law shall not depart from your mouth, but you shall meditate on it day and night, so that you may be careful to do according to all that is written in it. For then you will make your way prosperous, and then you will have good success.*

Again, whatever it is you believe, know that our subconscious mind can lead to prosperity and success when we focus on the positives. When we use our imagination, desire, and faith to be our daily, primary focus, God, the universe, your faith will lead you to prosperity and good success in your business, in your home, and in your life.

Luke 24:38 ESV: *And he said to them, "Why are you troubled, and why do doubts arise in your hearts?*

When your subconscious mind is focused on the positives, there is no need to be troubled and there is no room for doubt. I am not saying to ignore things that appear negative that happen in our lives. Remember, it is not the situation; it is how we see the situation and the subconscious thoughts we have about our circumstances that can either be viewed as negative or as an opportunity to learn, grow, and to transform.

The serenity prayer can also help with our subconscious mind: Accept the things we cannot change, change the things we can, and know the difference. With that kind of attitude contained in our subconscious mind, it will ease worry, discontent and any other negative as a result of what we may be experiencing.

1 Corinthians 13:4-7 ESV: *Love is patient and kind; love does not envy or boast; it is not arrogant or rude. It does not insist on its own way; it is not irritable or resentful; it does not rejoice at wrongdoing but rejoices with the truth. Love bears all things, believes all things, hopes all things, endures all things.*

Just imagine, if we allowed our subconscious mind to focus on love, our lives, our families, our society, and our world would be a far better place. Imagine allowing our subconscious mind to focus on love— unconditional love—there would be less sickness, less strife, and no hate towards ourself or others.

Again, our subconscious mind is in full operation all day and all night. Some things we can do to change our way of thinking include affirmations, meditation, reading self-help books and, of course, standing on your faith. As a Christian, I find the Bible to be a GREAT source for feeding my subconscious mind. Thinking about certain scriptures allows me to focus on the positive and on the promises of God.

VERA THOMAS

About Vera Thomas: Vera Thomas lives in the state of Georgia. She is, to date, a four-times bestselling author, podcast host, certified transformation coach, family mediator, and Classroom Management Advocate, Trainer, Speaker, as well as a Poet. She works with parents, children, schools, organizations and churches.

Vera's life story directed her towards working with organizations that provided hope and empowerment to people like her to better themselves. It is her goal to help others overcome a circumstance that diminishes and help them to surge ahead with their dreams. Vera graduated *Cum Laude* with a Bachelor's in psychology from Walsh University in Canton, OH.

Vera's work as a facilitator for more than three decades and includes developing training programs for youth and adults. Hear her story and think about your own. Vera is available for companies who want to transform their teams or individuals who want to transform their lives.

Author's Website: *www.linktr.ee/VeraThomasInstillingGreatness*

Book Series Website: *www.The13StepsToRiches.com*

Yuri Choi

HOW TO ACTUALLY CHANGE YOUR SUBCONSCIOUS MIND

What if I told you there is a deeper programming of your mind that is running underneath your conscious mind that is dictating how you perceive everything in the world? What if the reality that we think we share is only as similar as the set of subconscious beliefs that we share and actually has nothing to do with what we see, hear, or otherwise take in as sensory input?

What if I told you that, through the feeling and the meaning that we put through the lens of the subconscious mind, this world is actually open for interpretation and is neutral? What if I told you that, although the subconscious programming of your mind does exist, there are ways that you can shift even your most deeply ingrained beliefs about the world for you to have a richer and more expansive life?

What if I reminded you that you are that capable and powerful?

As a Performance Coach for high achievers and entrepreneurs, I have helped many clients of mine change these deeply rooted beliefs that direct their reality in the background. In this chapter, I'd like to offer a few practical tools you can use to start working on shifting your subconscious beliefs towards expansion.

Shift Your Fun Blockers into Fun Amplifiers

In my coaching practice, I have coined the term "fun blockers" for any set of subconscious beliefs that get in the way of having the most fun, joy, and abundance in our lives and business. These are often the set of beliefs that keep us in a limited, scarcity, or fear-base mindset that leads us to contracting rather than expanding.

I've found that one of the most common and fundamental *fun blockers* that many hold is the variation of this statement: "I am not enough." And this offers many variations of *fun blockers,* such as, "I am not smart enough," "I am not rich enough," "I am not skilled enough," and the list goes on. One of the ways that you can make these *fun blockers* in your subconscious mind turn into *fun amplifiers* is to switch the statement to the total opposite, so that it becomes an expansive affirmation that can help overcome the *fun blocker.*

For instance, for "I am not good enough," the obvious opposite of this would be, "I am enough." But to really reprogram our mind and amplify the fun, we can try on the affirmation of, "I am whole and beautiful." While this may not seem as if it is the exact opposite of a statement at a glance, it *amplifies* the fun and joy by reading it, and helps us overcome our *fun blockers.*

When you repeat this statement as an affirmation, my invitation for you is to start remembering one piece of evidence in your life where you did actually feel "whole" and "beautiful." Maybe even start writing these down in a journal. With practice, as Napoleon Hill says, we can reprogram our subconscious mind through *auto-suggestions.*

The Key is Shifting How You Get to Feel

Now, as you read this, the critic in your mind might jump to the question of, "But does speaking these statements out loud actually work?" The critics of affirmations as a tool for shifting our deeper subconscious beliefs might want to know that there are two key components of making affirmations actually work for us.

The first key is to repeat the statements as many times as possible, and on a regular basis. It's just like any other physical exercise. A person who wishes to get a six-pack cannot possibly think that going to the gym for five days will magically give them a new set of abs. It takes *work.* It takes *discipline.* It takes *reps.* And *more reps.* Just like this is true for physical exercise, this is also true for our mental and emotional fitness. We get to put in the *reps* so that it starts to shift our mind.

The second key is to repeat these affirmations out loud, but also to practice what that statement actually feels like in our bodies. For example, if your new *fun activating statement* is "I am beautiful and whole," then as you say this out loud, even for a few seconds to minutes, take a deep breath and invoke the feeling in your body of feeling "beautiful" and "whole." If that is difficult to imagine at first, practice remembering what it felt like last time you felt "beautiful" and "whole." As you practice the *feeling* behind these words, this amplifies the effect of these affirmations.

Create & Maintain an Abundant Mindset by Shifting Your Language

As a writer, poet, and person who believes that words all carry specific and unique vibrational frequency, I am very careful about the words that construct my reality around me. One reason these affirmations are really powerful is that when we design these *fun amplifying statements,* we get to consciously choose the words that orbit in our reality on a daily basis. By switching out a few words that do not serve us and adding a few very expansive words, your subconscious mind can shift rapidly and massively.

For instance, whenever I hear my clients say, "I need" or "I should," I call them out. These words such as *need* or *should* are directly tied to scarcity, lacking, and limited subconscious beliefs. The statement "I need" shows that your brain has just searched for what's missing, and what's not already abundant. "I should " shows that your brain just scanned for how you're not doing enough or doing something right. Behind the layer of these words, it infers that we are not abundant and that we are not enough. It is projecting that there is a need, meaning we are not whole and content as we are, and it also projects a set of unnecessary expectations upon ourselves or others.

Instead, try on expansive words and statements such as "I am grateful that…" or "I am blessed that…" It may sound cheesy at first, but over time, as you shift your language, you will start to see that it can massively shift the direction of your subconscious mind from lacking and scarcity to expansive and powerful.

These are some powerful practical tools, although shared in bits and pieces, that can help you, if you decide to actually infuse these into your daily life. Among other powerful tools that I offer, my clients also enjoy being coached in staying accountable to these subtle to more significant changes that can shift the deeper programming of their minds.

I hope that these tools start to activate your thought processes on which deeper beliefs you are ready to shed, and how possible it is that we can shift these programming that drive our behaviors, emotions, and mental processes. By becoming aware of and starting to utilize these tools to shift your mindset, they can have a drastic and positive impact in your life and business in big ways—if you allow them.

Journaling Questions:

1. What are some *fun blockers,* or beliefs in your subconscious mind that keep you limited, that you can start to become aware of and shed?

2. If those fun blockers were no longer a part of your subconscious mind, what could become possible for you?

3. What "I should…" statements do you use throughout the day that keep you in a scarcity mindset? Can you write them down to become aware?

4. What would feeling "whole" and "beautiful" feel like in your body?

5. How would living in this feeling dominantly change your subconscious mind potentially?

YURI CHOI

About Yuri Choi: Yuri is Founder of Yuri Choi Coaching. Choi is a performance coach for entrepreneurs and high achievers. She helps them create and stay in a powerful, abundant, unstoppable mindset to achieve their goals by helping them gain clarity and understanding, leverage their emotional states, and create empowering habits and language patterns.

She is a speaker, writer, creator, connector, YouTuber, and the author of Creating Your Own Happiness. Choi is passionate about spreading the messages about meditation, power of intention, and creating a powerful mindset to live a fulfilling life. She is also a Habitude Warrior Conference Speaker and emcee, and she is also a designated guest coach for Psych2Go, the largest online mental health magazine and YouTube Channel.

Her mission in the world is to inspire people to live leading with L.O.V.E. (which stands for: laughter, oneness, vulnerability, and ease) and to ignite people's souls to live in a world of infinite creative possibilities and abundance.

Author's Website: *www.YuriChoiCoaching.com*

Book Series Website: *www.The13StepsToRiches.com*

GRAB YOUR COPY OF AN OFFICIAL PUBLICATION
WITH THE ORIGINAL UNEDITED TEXT FROM 1937
BY THE NAPOLEON HILL FOUNDATION!

THE NAPOLEON HILL FOUNDATION
WWW.NAPHILL.ORG

Habitude Warrior Mastermind

Join a team of
AWESOME
Entrepreneurs, Coaches, Business Owners, and Leaders to support you in your journey of success!

Be one of my personal guests for a session!
www.MastermindGuestPass.com

HABITUDE WARRIOR & INTEGRITY PUBLISHING EDITORIAL TEAM

Habitude Warrior International and Integrity Publishing take great pride in our editorial team who put their sweat, tears, and heart into each and every project and national bestseller! Thank you team!

JON KOVACH JR.
Team Manager

Jon Kovach Jr. strives to assist every author and every team member in the process of self-development for ultimate success.

PAT MINTON
VP of Operations

Pat Minton has been with the Habitude Warrior International team for over 20 years getting her start with Brian Tracy & Erik Swanson.

JILLIAN KOVACH
Editorial Manager

Jillian is a vital team member of Habitude Warrior & Integrity Publishing bringing her expertise managing our Editorial Department.

FATIMA HURD
Editorial Team & Photographer

Fatima is our Professional Photographer for Habitude Warrior as well as one of our members on the Proofing Department team.

LAUREN COBB
Editorial Team Member

Lauren Cobb is part of our Proofing Department for Habitude Warrior & Integrity Publishing as well as one of our authors.

To inquire about joining our team please send us an email to Team@HabitudeWarrior.com

.

www.ingramcontent.com/pod-product-compliance
Lightning Source LLC
Chambersburg PA
CBHW051301120626
46547CB00015B/2031